A GHOSTLY GUIDE
TO
TENNESSEE

BY

JAMES FOSTER ROBINSON

CONTENTS

INTRODUCTION

I created this guide for those who are interested in ghosts, whether they believe in them or not. This guide is NOT an in-depth investigation of haunted places but an introduction to the many ghosts of Tennessee. As such, I have not elaborated on each ghostly appearance, but gave you just enough detail to pique your morbid curiosity.

The ghosts told about here are from legends, tales and reported sightings from citizens of Tennessee and others. I have not been able to ascertain whether or not they are true, nor will I try. I will leave that to the "professional" ghost hunters and the experts. I present them here solely for interest's sake and morbid curiosity.

I have arranged the stories by region and then by counties and then by communities alphabetically.

Lock your doors and turn on all your lights but one to read by. Sit down in a comfortable chair, and start reading. If you hear strange sounds, pay no attention. Keep on reading. If you see something out of the corner of you eye, ignore it. Just keep on reading. You might be ok... maybe... Just maybe!!!

One final note. If you are the owner of any property mentioned in this book and do not wish to have any story about your property printed in future editions of this book, please contact me by email at jamesfosterrobinson@live.com. As I am both the author and publisher and publish the book online through createspace.com and amazon.com, I can made changes as necessary.

REGIONS OF TENNESSEE

There are three geographically and culturally distinct grand divisions in the State of Tennessee - East Tennessee, Middle Tennessee and West Tennessee. The ghost stories are arranged according to county and region.

EAST TENNESSEE

East Tennessee is a name given to approximately the eastern third of the state. It has thirty three counties, thirty of which are within the Eastern Time Zone and the other three counties, Bledsoe, Cumberland and Marion, in the Central Time Zone. The region lies within the Appalachian Mountains with densely forested, six thousand foot high mountains and broad river valleys.

COUNTIES

ANDERSON COUNTY

BRICEVILLE

Briceville is an community in Anderson County and has a train bridge in the lower end over Coal Creek. The main industry was coal mining and nearly everyone was employed in it. The ghost of a young black miner named Dick Drummond walks from one end of the bridge to the other before disappearing. If you listen carefully, you can hear the sound of a noose swinging in the breeze. There are two stories explaining how Dick came to be there. One relates that the KKK, active in the village years ago, hung Dick off the bridge for some unknown reason. The other tells about a revolt by miners when they were replaced by the coal company with cheap prison labor. The State Militia were called in to stop the revolt and poor Dick was hung from the bridge. Other miners were killed during some of the fighting.

Wait, there is still more ghosts to tell about. About 1900, one hundred and eighty-four men were killed in the Fraterville Mine Disaster on Coal Creek at Briceville. On quiet nights, when the moon is full, you can hear the screams of the long dead miners.

OAK RIDGE

Oak Ridge is a city partly in Anderson County and and partly in Roane county about twenty-five miles west of Knoxville.

The Alexander Inn, if it still exists, was said to be haunted. When you approached the building, you could see a ghostly figure staring out through the curtains in one of the windows. Inside, the walls were covered with blood and the floors with broken glass. Then there were disembodied footsteps overhead upstairs. It was apparently a very unpleasant place to visit.

Several people were murdered near the George Jones Missionary Church on Galaher Road in Oak Ridge. Some thing or someone disembodied follows visitors thriugh the area after dark. There have been unconfirmed reports of strange accidents happening to people who linger in the area late at night.

The small Wheat Community Church with its small graveyard has apparently been closed for many years. In the 1940's, the minister hung himself in the bell tower after going insane. Local legend claims that people, who have ventured there on Halloween, have seen the noose swinging in the Bell Tower and blood dripping from it! That is what they say! Blood dripping from the swinging rope! Be aware that the place is apparently posted "NO TRESPASSING! If you are bold enough to try entering the property, do not expect me to post your bail.

OLIVER SPRINGS

Oliver Springs is a town partly in Anderson, Morgan, and Roane counties. There was an old abandoned barn in the town where a little girl playing the attic of the barn fell and died. They said that you could hear strange noises in the back of the building like finger nails scratching on something. Some, who had entered the barn, claimed that they felt someone was staring at them. And, wouldn't you know it, they saw blood red eyes at the back of the barn staring right at them. I do not know if that barn, said to be in the center of town, is still standing.

The Colonial Hall is located in the Roane County part of Oliver Springs. An unknown little girl died there many years ago but still complains about being cold while walking up and down the hall stairs.

BLEDSOE COUNTY

PIKEVILLE

Pikeville is a city in and the county seat of Bledsoe County. An old broken down house sits on the top of a hill above the Mount Crest Church of God in Pikeville. On a rainy day, people say that you can hear an invisible carriage coming down the road and then disembodied screams and the terrified cries of horses. A family of four were killed there many years ago when their carriage crashed off the road at the bluff above the old house. They also say that when driving by the old house, you may experience the unsettling feeling of something or someone watching you. Was there and maybe still is something in that house that spooked the horses and caused the accident?

BLOUT COUNTY

ALCOAl

Alcoa is a city in Blount County south of Knoxville. There is an old stone house where a couple used to live that has an interesting legend attached to it. Apparently the husband and wife believed that as long as they continued to work on the house they would live for ever. When his wife died, he simply claimed that she had lost faith. After working on the house for forty-five years, the old man past away. It seems he is still trying to keep his faith even after dying for they say that you can see a candle burring in a window and hear him still building inside the house anytime during the day or night.

MARYVILLE

Maryville is the county seat of Blount County and is located tweny miles south of Knoxville. The Carpenters School in Maryville is said to have been built on the site of an old cemetery and is haunted by a little girl who is often heard crying but not seen in the school's hallways. Children playing outside have reported that other ghosts often would grab their arms and try to take them away. The children quickly found a way to prevent this. If they did not look at the ghosts, the specters left them alone.

A shy lady named Lily, who was left by her lover for the star of show, haunts the theater at Maryville College. She has been seen wearing her favorite black and white dress as she walks along the catwalks above the stage.

Years ago, a man apparently hung himself in the boy's locker room in the gym of Maryville's

Porter Elementary School. It seems he may haunt it. A light in a locker room closet goes off and on seemingly by itself and the toilet flushes of its own accord. You think there may just be something wrong with both the light and the toilet? Maybe.

BRADLEY COUNTY

CHARLESTON

The city of Charleston in Bradley County has a famous ghost known as the Phantom Monk. In 1867, a flood in Charleston washed away part of the railway tracks and a train crashed into a ravine as a result. All but one of the bodies from that tragedy except that of a monk from Baltimore was found and buried. Later it turned out that a local doctor had found the monk's body and had taken it to his office where he stripped the flesh from the skeleton, bleached the skeleton and hung it in his office. Apparently the monk's spirit did not like it and haunted the doctor's office for years. In 1932 the old building was torn down and replaced with a new building. Workers at that time found a rosary and a monk's robe hanging in between the walls. They say that the ghost of the monk still hangs out in the new building and sometimes walks the tracks where the train wrecked. Perhaps he is looking for his rosary and robe? Does anyone know where they are or where his skeleton went to? If found, the

Phantom Monk may find some peace.

CLEVELAND

The city of Cleveland is the county seat of Bradley County. Local legend claims that on the eve of October 30th no one should go near the Greens Cavern at midnight. If you do and you see a tall shadowy form carrying a sickle, you risk losing your soul to it. The shadowy figure will take it back to its cave and your soul will be lost for ever.

There is or was a mausoleum in the yard of St. Luke's Episcopal Church in the center of town. A little girl named Nina, an only children of the Craigmiles Family who passed away in a tragic accident, was buried there. They say that there is a pink streak above the door that appeared just after her burial there and can not be removed. They say that the streak bleeds every year on the anniversary of her death. The apparition of a young child dressed in 1800's style clothing has been seen near the mausoleum. The sound of crying has also been heard.

CAMPBELL COUNTY

CARYVILLE

The town of Caryville in Campbell County

has at least two good ghost hauntings. A red half-goat half-human creature nearly eight feet tall and with a very distinctive pentagram on its fore head has been spotted a number of times along a ten mile stretch near the Red Ash Cemetery. Some motorist who saw it tried to get away from it by driving over a train track crossing only to be confronted by a ten foot wide blue light hovering over the rail crossing. I assume they were able to away from the light, as they apparently lived to tell the tale.

Fifty years ago, a man fell off the Red Ash Coal Towers at Caryville. His apparition is often seen falling off them time and time again. His ghostly presence or that of some other passed on person is often felt in the depot office while furniture has moved around the room by itself. There are also rumors that a ghost train often comes down the now unused tracks.

JELLICO

Years ago, a peeping tom, caught by the police while he was wandering in the Bluff Springs apartment complex in the city of LaFollette, was killed along with two police officers when the police cruiser crashed. Now at 1:23 AM every night, the residents of that complex are treated to the terrifying sight of red glowing eyes and strange sounds like movements outside their apartments.

CARTER COUNTY

ELIZABETHTON

The community of Elizabeth is the county seat of Carter County. Granny February, a local legend, is supposedly buried in Arney Hill Cemetery. I do not know why she is legendary but it is claimed that if you visit her grave at midnight on Halloween and listen carefully you will hear Granny February rocking her rocking chair.

The Gwendolyn House, built in the early 1900's, sits just off Bristol Highway at Elizabethton. The building is haunted by number of spooks, including a little girl, a woman who tells the living to get out just before she disappears and even some ghost dogs. Are the ghost dogs still guarding their ghostly owners.

There is a tragic story told about a steel bridge in Elizabethton, possibly the Watauga Bridge. A young couple meeting under the bridge one night were attacked and robbed. They were both stabbed. The girl died on the spot but the boy was able to escape up onto the roadway. There he flagged down a car and jumped into the back seat for help. It is not reported whether or not he survived his wound. But it is told that if you drive a car over that bridge at midnight on Halloween and stop in the middle of it, someone unseen will get into your back seat even if all your doors are locked. How do you know that someone is there? There will be a depression in the seat as if someone was seating there. Of course, you will not see anyone. To add to the macabre atmosphere of the place, a strange figure in monk's robe is said to wander the area after dark. If you get close enough to see its face under the hood, you will be shocked by the terrifying view of a skull! Maybe you do not want to get that close as the creature is said to be a spirit of pure evil.

ROAN MOUNTAIN

This is the story of the Phantom Jumper of Dark Hollow. A small cemetery lies on Dark Hollow Road just outside of Roan Mountain in rural Carter County. Many of the graves there are unmarked. In one of these unmarked graves lies a Mr. Jenkins. Some people believe that a lady named Delinda shares Mr. Jenkins' grave. Here's why.

Around 1900, Delinda was known for having many lovers, some of whom were married to other women. These other women did not like Delinda and would have like to stop her antics. Somehow Delinda became sick. Then most of the men in the community also fell sick. The good ladies of the community then decided it was time to do some thing drastic. They marched to Delinda's house to teach her a lesson. Alas, the lady in question was not home. The ladies on a mission decided that she had left. And, what do you know, Delinda was never seen again. Well maybe!

You see, Delinda favorite lover, Mr. Jankins, died that same day when he accidentally shot himself with a loaded rifle that he thought was unloaded. His wife had apparently load it and forgot to tell him. So they say! Delinda never appeared in person at her lover's funeral. One mourner thought he saw a shadowy form lurking near the casket. The pall bearers then found that the casket seemed very heavy when they carried it to the grave as if there were two people in it. Of course, no one thought to look inside just to make sure. To this day, some people believe that Delinda somehow climbed into her lover's casket and was buried with him. As I said earlier, Delinda was never seen again and that made a lot of local women happy.

That is not the end of the story. There has to be a ghostly part to it. If you drive by that cemetery late at night, you sometimes may feel a bump on your car as if someone had leaped onto the back of it. Local lore claims that it id Delinda - the Phantom Jumper of Dark Hollow who is trying to get away from that graveyard. Why? She did not get a Christian burial and is restless wanting to get out of the place. Or, maybe she is tired of her lover and is looking for a new one!

Morgan Branch Cemetery is not far from the Dark Hollow Road Cemetery just outside Roan Mountain in Carter County. This mysterious and crowded cemetery has a mixture of old and new graves. It is thought that some of the graves are on top of older graves and that seems to be causing a problem. Strange things happen there. Weird noises have been heard. Strange lights such as the famous orbs have been sighted. Photos taken at different times showed unusual disturbances and orbs.

CLAIBORNE COUNTY

HARROGATE

The city of Harrogate in Claiborne County is just across the border from Middlesboro, Kentucky. Lincoln Memorial University there is haunted by several phantoms. Grant Lee Dormitory at the university was apparently a Hotel and sanitarium in the 1890's. The building back then burnt to the ground in a fire. Two people, a woman wearing a red dress and her child staying on the fourth floor, were the only victims. In the 1960's, the building once again burnt to the ground. A woman in a red dress was spotted calling for help from a fourth floor window. Nobody was apparently found and no one was reported missing. No one knew who the lady in the red dress was. To this day, residents of the dormitory have heard and some times seen the lady in the red dress running up the stairs and down the fourth floor hall.

A man dressed all in black appears before staff's startled eyes at the radio station at Lincoln Memorial University. No one seems to know who he is, where he comes from and where he disappears to.

COCKE COUNTY

NEWPORT

Newport on Interstate 40 is a city in and also the county seat of Cocke County. Back in the 1970's, a plane crashed in nearby Parrotsville killing nearly seventy people. The Memorial Building in Newport was used to store the bodies until they could be buried. In the year 2000, some college students, doing a research paper for their Psychology class, decided to use the Memorial Building as their subject. Apparently, people had complained that scary things happened there. Well, the students got a lot of data for the paper. The disembodied scream of a woman was heard in the attic. A little boy with a bowl hair cut appeared in front of a male student and seemed startled to see the student. The boy, seating Indian style, tilted his head and started to scream. Another student caught on film a shadow dashing by him and also the ghostly specter of a man standing right behind him. I wonder if they got an "A" on their Psychology paper. Other visitors to the building have felt strong unseen presences, heard disembodied voices and babies crying as well as a woman screaming.

CUMBERLAND COUNTY

CROSSVILLE

Crossville is a city in and the county seat of Cumberland County. There is apparently another haunted road and hill at Mile Marker Ten on Interstate 40. Years ago, a bus with kids broke down on the slope of the hill and a tractor trailer coming fast over the crest crashed into the bus killing everyone on it. Now if you put your vehicle in neutral when you get to the hill, he ghosts of the children will push you up and over the crest to safety and out of the way of oncoming traffic. And when you check the back of your car, you will find the hand prints of the ghostly children on the truck. Or so they say! But remember the road is busy and you hazard an accident if you try this stunt.

If you are driving along Interstate 40 just outside Crossville and near the Obed River, you may be startled by a bruch of strange lights bobbing along. They may even cross the highway in front of you. They are the Cumberland Mountains Ghost Lights. They are not as well known as the Chapel Hill Lights but many people have reported seeing them. They are supposedly the spirits of two robbers and an old trapper they were trying to steal from. They got into a fight in his cabin just a few feet from where Interstate 40 is now and knocked over an oil lamp setting the cabin on fire. All three died in the blaze but now wander around the area in the form of the Cumberland Mountain Ghost Lights.

GRASSY COVE

Grassy Cove, a community just south of Crossville in Cumberland County near the Roane County line, lies in a quiet little valley. Once upon a time, this community held a dark secret. Saltpeter was dug up in many caves and mines in the area during the Civil War. A couple of years after the war, some boys found the petrified body of a man. It was taken to the local coroner's office. When no one claimed it, the body was buried in the Methodist Cemetery in Grassy Cove. That was when things started to act up. At night moans were heard coming from the grave where the petrified body was interred. Disembodied screams startled people on the road passing the cemetery church. Many became too frightened to attend that church.

The local gravedigger had warned them not to bury the body. He then got the chore of returning the body to the caves. He did but told no one which cave the body was now residing in. If you explore the caves in that area and find a petrified body, I strongly suggest that you do not disturb it, leave immediately and tell no one about it.

GRAINGER COUNTY

WASHBURN

The Arnwine Cemetery in the community of Washburn in rural northern Grainger County sits about a dozen miles on a narrow old back road. The cemetery has apparently not been used for burials since 1903. If you visit it, you might see the apparition of an unknown woman and you car may not start easily.

GREENE COUNTY

GREENVILLE

Greenville is a town in Greene County and the county seat of Greene County. There was an old arch railway bridge in rural Greenville that may be demolished now. According to local legend, over one hundred years ago, many a lynching occurred there. A number of slaves and free blacks suffered vigilante justice there. Their spirits are said to have haunted the bridge and may still haunt the area where the bridge was. In addition to the sightings of specters, there is the disembodied sounds of voices and splashes in the water.

Years ago, a young girl named Ryan was killed in her house on Robin Hood Road in Greenville. They say that her remains are still buried in the basement and that Ryan roams the area seeking help in uncovering the details of her death. Strange things such as the lights turning and on, blinds opening and closing and objects moving around by themselves occur in Ryan's old house. If you are lucky enough to be invited inside that house (if it still exists) you just might make the acquaintance of the young Ryan.

Tusculum College in Greenville has at least two ghostly residents. The Doak house on the outskirts of the campus is now a museum. It has a very unusual audial exhibit. The haunting sounds of a piano or organ came be heard coming from the empty upstairs. It is not known who or what is playing the invisible instrument. Virginia Hall on the campus was once an all female dormitory. Years ago, the dorm caught fire and the head mother who lived on the top floor never made it out. Now you can hear her frightening screams coming from the sealed top floor. It is also said that

Katherine Hall has some ghostly activity but what, I have not found out. It too was an all girls dorm. One of the young girls there had a baby which was taken by the head mother. The girl took the baby back after killing the head mother. The baby must have died as it is said that its body is buried under the building. Does the ghost of the baby cry out for its mother or does the murdered head mother seek revenge?

HAMBLEN COUNTY

RUSSELLVILLE

Russellvile, a small village in Hamblen County, has at least one ghost resident. The company, now known as Morristown Block, was once called Vaughn Block. Years ago, the owner was said to have had an affair with the company secretary. The secretary apparently killed herself but speculation had it that the owner killed her because she was pregnant. Late night workers at the company now hear what sounds like a struggle between a man and a woman and then silence. When they checked, there was no sign of anyone or a struggle. Now that secretary used to live across the street and her spirit has been seen there. She does not bother anyone but seems to be watching for someone or something.

HAMILTON COUNTY

CHATTANOOGA

Chattanooga, the fourth-largest city in Tennessee, is the seat of Hamilton County and has at least four ghost stories. Across from Greenwood Cemetery is a pond or quarry. This pond is supposedly quite deep with steep sides and underwater caverns. A man and his invalid wife lived in a nearby house. When he fell in love with another woman, he decided to get rid of his wife by pushing her in her wheel chair into the pond. That is how the legend of the Lady of the Lake was born. Visitors to the area often see a green mist out on the water that comes into shore. In the mist is a beautiful woman with all her faculties and walking on two good legs. Then the mist disappears and the marks of a wheelchair on found on the shore of that haunted pond.

Memorial Park, one of the largest cemeteries in Tennessee, is just off Memorial Drive in Chattanoga. One of the most beautiful cemeteries in Hamilton County, it has graves dating back to the 1800's. This cemetery is said to be home to a "Black Aggie". What? Do not know what a "Black Aggie" is? Well I will tell you. A "Black Aggie" is a dark form that appears in cemeteries and other places, performing the same task over and over again. This B.A. (short for "Black Aggie") hangs out under an arch in the graveyard. No one knows why. There is a theory that the family of a man who wanted an arch place over his grave thought it was a silly idea. When the man died, the family had an arch installed at the entrance to their family plot. The ghost of the man, upset that the arch was not placed over his grave, hangs out under the family arch. Maybe he is trying to make the best of the situation. Maybe. It is only a theory.

One of Chattanooga's greatest landmarks is the Radisson Read House Hotel at 827 Broad Street. Opened in 1847, it was then the Crutchfield House. During the Civil War, it was the center of conflict between Union and Confederate sympathizers. When the hotel was under Union control, apparently a Union soldier's killing a prostitute in Room 311 was covered up. The hotel burnt down in 1867 and was rebuilt. That room 311 is said to be haunted. Bizarre apparitions have been spied in it and strange sounds have been heard coming from that room which is only used upon request of a guest. Most guests, requesting the haunted room, do not stay long in it. Is the room haunted by the murdered prostitute, the soldier who killed her and now suffers remorse for eternity or both?

HARRISON

Harrison Bay is near the community of Harrison in Hamilton County. The story goes that an albino man named Patsy, who lived in a cabin near Harrison Bay, was thought to have murdered several people there. It is not known if he was ever charged with the crimes. Now, red eyes and no obvious body are often seen floating through the nearby woods. Are they the eyes of the murder seeking another victim or a victim looking for some payback?

SALE CREEK

Sale Creek is a small community in northern Hamilton County. For over one hundred years, a glowing white specter has joined uninvited many hay and horse back rides in the area from Shipley Hollow to the Mill Dam on Daughtery Ferry Road off Highway 27.

SIGNAL MOUNTAIN

A very unusual ghost story is told about Mabitt Springs at Signal Mountain in Hamilton County. Late a night, campers in a nearby woods have spied a lone campfire off in the trees. When they investigate it, they hear someone calling their name. Then they see a dead-looking grey hand extend out through the flaps of a spooky looking tent. Then the hand disappears back inside and a little boy with no legs will pull himself out of the tent. Don't listen to him. Get out of there! If you listen it will tell a woeful story begging you to stay with him in the woods forever. Be careful as he will try to drag himself closer to you to do the devil knows what! Some say that if he touches your face, it will start to eat you. True or now, I, for one, do not intend to find out!

The old Signal Mountain Elementary School, now apparently a community center, had a loft in one of its class rooms. The loft was home to a phantom of a little girl dressed in an old school uniform, who sobbed "My dolly! My little rag dolly! It's burning!" It is not known if she is still there in the present community center, crying her eyes out.

MORRISTOWN

Bethesda Church and cemetery is in Morristown, the county seat of Hamblem County and is said to be haunted by Confederate soldiers from the Civil War as well as a phantom of a woman. The ghost soldiers are unfriendly to visitors especially those with a northern accent. The boarded up church, used as a hospital during the Civil War, supposedly contains more lost souls who can not get out of the building. The woman weeps for her daughter who died the day she was born. Both parents and the baby are buried in a family plot. Many visitors have heard her weeping and have seen strange things happen around the grave site. Unfortunately, the witnesses failed to record what those strange things were.

OOLTEWAH

The Super 8 Motel in the community of Ooltewah in Hamilton County is said to be haunted by the ghost of a twenty year old girl who was murdered there. She has been seen sitting on the edge of the bed, seemingly undressing. I hope her disappears before she finishes undressing. It could be embarrassing for couple renting the room.

HANCOCK COUNTY

I have not found any ghost stories for this county as yet. If you know any please email me at jamesfosterrobinson@live.com and I will include it in any future volume or revision. Type GHOST in the subject heading so I will not miss it.

HAWKINS COUNTY

CHURCHILL

People have been seeing imp like creatures

wandering fields on Halloween in Church Hill, a community in Hawkins County. They have been described as looking like cows but with red eyes and a possessed look to them. Do cows' eyes look red at night when you shine a light in them? Maybe. To me, cows always look like they are possessed until they are milked.

SURGOINSVILLE

The town of Surgoinsville in Hawkins County has a ghost dog in a cemetery there. The New Providence Church Cemetery sits just off Highway 11W in Surgoinsville. Visitors to the place at night have heard phantom footsteps walking along with them and some have seen a black dog by the grave of Captain Maxwell. The dog just disappears into thin air when approached. A tree called the Old White Oak sits in the yard and is the spot where a family and their dog was murdered. Now ghostly figures are seen there and disembodied voices are heard by those who listen carefully. That poor tree has been nicked named "Booger Oak".

There is more about that black dog. Some feel it may be the legendary Long Dog. This ghostly canine has been seen after dark along the roads around Surgoinsville looking for its lost master. Many feel that the Long Dog is the family pet killed with that family under the Old White Oak over one hundred years ago. The critter is very long and ghostly. It used to run along side of wagons and occasionally jump on board as if looking for someone. I wonder if it has tried to jump on cars and trucks lately.

JEFFERSON COUNTY

DANDRIGE

Dandridge is a town in and the county seat of Jefferson County. The Dandridge Tennessee Mountain Inn has a ghostly guest, a little girl who walks the balcony at night. One guest apparently caught her on film. I would like to see that photo.

JEFFERSON

A girl, long passed away, has been seen walking around the attic of a house on the old AJ Highway at Jefferson City. This phantom is so solid that she even casts a shadow. Might the house be the Glenmore Mansion just off AJ Highway? An unexplained light is often seen at night in the attic of the mansion.

Another home in Jefferson City is haunted by the ghostly of a woman who screams on the stairs. Window shutters open and close by themselves and spectral images manifest in mirrors.

Often unexplained gun shots are heard. It was the Colonial Inn during the Civil War and then the Jefferson City Inn before it became a private home. Years ago, a man's wife pushed him down the stairs killing him, another man shot himself in the Kitchen and a slave girl hung herself in the basement. Do the souls of these unfortunate folk still hang around the once upon Inn?

The students in a certain class room in Jefferson County High School in Jefferson City complain about cold air always coming from a closet in the room. In addition, scratch marks are always appearing on that closet door. What is going on here? Are the kids making the scratch marks? Is there a hole in the closet allowing the cold air through, apparently even in summer? Local rumor claims that a girl was raped and murdered in that closet. Maybe it is haunted. What do you think?

Coaches and gym teachers at Jefferson Middle School, formerly Jefferson High School years ago, often hear basketballs being bounced in the gym late at night when they are alone correcting papers. Are they alone? Could it be the ghost of a female basketball player who was in a car crash on the way to a school dance? Did she love basketball so much that she did not want to give it up even in the afterlife?

JOHNSON COUNTY

MOUNTAIN CITY

There is a strange sight seen often on Doe Mountain near Mountain City. A fireball know as the Doe Mountain Fireball rolls up and down the mountain slopes crossing dry leaves without setting anything on fire. The strange object varies from the size of a bowling ball to one nearly three feet in diameter. No logical explanation has been found for it. Is it a ghost or just an example of the mysterious ball lightning?

Prospect Hill Bed & Breakfast in Mountain City has been the scene of some strange activity. Bathroom glasses fly though the air and shatter. A shadow is often seen disappearing around a corner while the sound of leather shoes is heard going up and down stairs. Then there is the invisible baby that cries from time to time.

NEVA

A little boy haunted the bathroom at Neva School in the small community of Neva in Johnson County. He was bullied a lot there and ran away one day never to be found again. But his ghost remembered and lingered there. I wonder if he is still there and if the building is still standing?

STONE MOUNTAIN

Fiddler's Rock is an overhang atop Stone Mountain in Johnson County. The ghost of the famous Martin Stone can be heard playing a fiddle followed by loud screaming. Martin used to like to climb up there with his fiddle and a shotgun. He would attract rattlesnakes with his fiddle playing and then blast them with his shotgun. One day, something went wrong. His body, covered with snake bites was found on that rock outcrop. His shot gun was nearby as was his fiddle. The snakes must not have liked his fiddle playing.

KNOX COUNTY

KNOXVILLE

The city of Knoxville is the county seat of Knox County. The Baker Peters Jazz Club in Knoxville, now a trendy Jazz bar, was once a Civil War era residence built by a Dr. James Harvey Baker. One of his sons fought for the Confederacy. The good doctor, while treating Confederate soldiers in his home, was shot and killed by Union soldiers when they occupied Knoxville. His son returned, killed the man who had informed on his father and was killed in returned by the informer's friends. Now, over a hundred years later, the good doctor is apparently still in the house he loved. The owner of the bar has a picture of his ghostly reflection and staff have felt chills, heard disembodied whispers and witnessed the unexplained movements of different objects around the building seemingly by themselves. Once, the candle holders on a candelabra in the dinning room were found twisted downward. It is also thought that the ghost of his son keeps the doctor company.

The Baptist Hospital in Knoxville is haunted by a number of spooks. The best known are two characters, Henry and Bob. You will find Henry hanging out in the Care Support office where he likes to play tricks such as hiding things. Henry, though mischievous, is friendly and will stop bothering you if you ask him nicely. Bob, also friendly, likes the ICU where he will opens and closes doors, throws papers around and turns the lights off and on. Once in awhile, he will put in a personal appearance.

The Bijou Theater in Knoxville is rumored to have a ghostly patron. He has been sighted several times and disembodied voices have been heard in the building which was a hospital years ago. Nothing much else is known about the haunting at this time.

Mysterious figures have been sighted prowling Churchill Road in a residential neighborhood of Knoxville. This is no description of these characters and no one claims to know who or what they are. It all might be dismissed as imagination or kids playing games but how do you explain the disembodied screaming that is sometimes heard?

Some wonderful things happened in the mid 1990's at the Copper Ridge Baptist Church. They were not ghostly manifestations but miracles. The church and the miracles were featured on the TV show "Unsolved Mysteries. On November 8th, 1995, lights in the form of crosses appeared in and around the church building. Word quickly spread of the miracle and soon thousands of people flocked to the small church to view the phenomena. Some people, suffering from incurable and terminal illnesses, were apparently cured on the spot. Pictures taken inside the church showed a bright white light, a man in a turban and other religious figures. Some visitors claimed to see with their own eyes Jesus and some angels. For awhile the church was open twenty four hours a day and seven days a week but is now apparently closed to the public. The name of the church has also been changed.

Elsewhere on Copper Ridge Road, they say there is an abandoned building that harbors evil. Many who have explored the site say that they felt a strong feeling of something menacing and evil. The two story building was in the past a Masonic

Lodge, a hospital in the Civil War and a church. One group of curious people left a tape recorder on in the building one night. When they retrieved it and played it back, they heard screams and strange sounds and then the sound of footsteps and that of the tape recorder clicking off. Others have reported seeing red eyes staring out of the windows at them and also dark forms moving around inside. Moans are often heard coming from the cemetery next door and strange lights and mist have occurred in the scary place. If all this is true, then evil does lurk in that building.

A Cracker Barrel Restaurant in Knoxville has a ghost as an employee. A waitress named Margie used to work there before she passed away. Apparently, she still pours coffee for customers and even receive tips. You will know if the waitress serving you is her as her name in on her name tag. They also say that when you go to use the phone in the back, you can hear a disembodied voice.

The First Presbyterian Church Cemetery is located in downtown Knoxville and is the oldest graveyard in Knoxville. There are mysteries about this church and you can read about them in Charles Edwin Price "Mysterious Knoxville". Even more interesting is the sighting of a "Black Aggie". This is the name given to a dark force that haunts cemeteries and other places. This Aggie, dark and wearing a hood while appearing semi-transparent, lurks around the cemetery late at night scaring unwanted visitors.

The Gay Street Bridge on Gay Street in Knoxville was the scene of a tragic hanging many years ago. A young man convicted of murder was hung from the third lantern in use at that time on the bridge. Just before he died, he claimed that if he was innocent, a sign on the bridge would show that they hung an innocent man. For many years, despite repairs, that third light apparently never worked. The bridge was closed down for awhile and then reopened. Reports have that the third light is now working. However, some say that the hung man's ghost walks that bridge late at night.

In the late 1970's, a young girl was badly injured when she was pushed down a stairs during an argument with her boyfriend at Knoxville's Halls High School. The boyfriend then took off leaving her there bleeding. Then he got nervous and returned to the scene of the argument and found that his girlfriend had disappeared. She was never seen again and the boyfriend apparently told no one about the incident. One year later, the boyfriend, returning home after a party, was stabbed and killed by someone unknown. Local legend claims that the dead girlfriend came back from the dead to avenge her death. Now strange and unnatural things happen in that tragic stairwell. The stairwell was finally closed up and not used any longer. Janitors working the night shift claimed to hear the couple arguing followed by the terrible sound of something falling down those boarded up stairs.

Hill Crest Nursing Home, once a TB Hospital, is known for its caring staff whether they are alive or passed away. They say that deceased staff members have been seen in Building B still doing their rounds.

An apartment complex, supposedly once home to the infamous Job Corp, not far from the University of Tennessee, has at least two creepy stories of a ghost or something evil haunting the place. The first woman to be convicted of murder and sentenced to death in the State of Tennessee was incarcerated there. Some feel that it is her ghost that roams this building. Strange, if it was her ghost, how could she be doing a haunting when she was still in jail awaiting execution. Others think that some sort of other evil lurks there and is responsible for evil people more evil. You might say then that evil made them do it.

The Lake Shore Asylum building in Knoxville, apparently now abandoned, was once part of the Lakeshore Mental Health Facility just off of Lyon's View Drive and like many such places seemed to attract many tales about it. Supposedly patients were mistreated there and their screams can still be heard as well as the sounds of shackles being thrown around. An unidentified evil entity is said to reside in that building which was used for satanic rituals in the 1970's. There was even an underground movie "St. Lucifer's" made about the supposed events occurring there.

Some of the houses in Knoxville's Lennox Place may be haunted. Not many of the owners are willing to talk about it. Can you blame them? The ghosts of a young lady with long blonde hair and a white haired old man in a long night gown like to visit the houses in the ghost so to speak and mischievously rattle dishes, unlock and open doors as well as garage doors in the middle of the night. This could severely disturb your sleep and lower your property values. Then, on the other hand, there is a growing market for haunted homes.

The Old Grey cemetery off Broadway in Knoxville is haunted by a mysterious black shape that sneaks among the tombstones late at night. This specter is thought to be one of the infamous "Black Aggies" that hang out in many cemeteries. No one knows who it is or why it is still this side of the veil.

Knoxville's University of Tennessee has a number of ghostly residents. Sophie abides in the 4th floor Resident's room in Stronberg Hall. She was one of the first female student to attend the

University and and puts in an appearance in the mirror in Stronmberg's lobby on her birthday. Strange noises are heard at night in the building. Residents are advised to refrain from sexual indiscretions as Sophie apparently does not approve.

Matin Clement Hall at U of T, the oldest building on the campus, is used as a dormitory when needed. The fourth floor, especially the community bathroom, is haunted by the ghost of a female student who killed herself on the premise.

The specter haunting the Hoskins Law Library at U of T is apparently "Evening Primrose" named after a short story of the same name by John Collier. She/he likes to occasionally knock books off the shelves and play games with the elevators. You will know she/he is there by the scent of cornbread and other sumptuous food she/he is cooking in her phantom kitchen. Disembodied footsteps have been heard in the stacks. You have probably guess by now that we are not sure of its gender. No one knows for sure who she/he was but some speculate that she/he was a poor graduate student hiding out in the Library while working on her/his dissertation. Maybe she/he liked it so well there that after she/he passed away in later life, she/he decided to still hang out in the library. It also may be a former director who still wanders around the campus long after he passed away.

The basement of U of T"s Tyson Alumni House is haunted. Staff working in the Alumni Affairs office have heard someone walking in the corridors but found no one when they checked. The disembodied spirit has also been blamed for low moans and with fiddling with the lights. The building was a grant from the Tyson Family who asked that the grave of their dog, Bonita, in the front yard be maintained. Many believe she is the specter haunting the house. There is also speculation that she might be the "Ghost Dog", a black, dog-like creature with dripping fangs that keeps watch for its master, a military general who resided in the area.

The Alumni Memorial Building is home to a ghost called Fanny. She feels she is an actress and often performs for visitors. Previously she hung about in the Science Building but moved to her present gig after the Science Building burnt to the ground in 1967. That building's auditorium had been used to put on plays. In the 1920's, Fanny had a small part in a movie made in Knoxville. The producers liked her and wanted her to come to Hollywood. She died before she could realize her dream.

Ralph is a friendly spirit who once roamed the Pi Kappa Fraternity House at the U of T during Chapter meetings and playing with the lights. It is not known if he is still there. Maybe he graduated to that great Ghost Fraternity House in the sky.

During the Civil War, the battle of Fort Summers occurred on U of T's campus and left a lasting impression. So much so that the specters of dead Union soldiers still patrol the campus while the disembodied sounds of marching and gun shots are heard at night. Most of the phantom action occurs on "the Hill" and also near apartments at Fifth Street and Lake Avenue. Are these apparitions the spirits of soldier killed in battle and never properly buried? The famous Wampus Cat has been seen on the Hill as well as a phantom wolf wandering the area calling out a low mournful howl. For more information on the Wampus Cat, check out my book "The Wampus Cat, Myth or Reality".

Reese Hall is said to have been build on an old cemetery and a Native American burial ground. The unhappy spirits of the dead buried there are said to show their displeasure in the halls of the building frightening residents.

Tyson Hall, home to the Lutheran Campus Ministries, is visited by the former owner in ghostly form.

A student committed suicide many years ago in Hess Hall and still hangs around there in ghostly form. It appears that McClung Museum was erected on the site of Indian Burial Mounds and the residence Native spirits are restless and wander the building as well as the Agricultural campus.

The Barbara Blount Hall, a woman's residence torn down in 1979, was haunted by Civil War soldiers that hung out in other parts of the campus.

Seven Islands Church, one of the oldest in Knox County, can be found on the French River in South Knoxville near the Sevier County line. Over the years, there has been ghostly activity both in the church and in the cemetery. The bell tower gives off sinister feelings and strange lights have been seen up there. Mysterious shadows, thought to belong to witches buried in the cemetery, are often spotted roaming the grounds.

POWELL

Powell is a community in Knox County. Black figures, possibly Black Aggies, have been seen moving around inside Copper Ridge Baptist Church. There is an old barn, or at least there was at one time, about one hundred yards from the church. Screams are heard coming from it and may be those of a young girl who was recorded on a tape recorder left on in the building one night asking for some one to "help us". You can also hear, they say, sounds of something or someone moving around the barn, then footsteps and then the tape turns off. As far as it known no one was in the building when the recording was made. The church was apparently torn down in 2007 or earlier.

LOUDON COUNTY

LENOIR CITY

Lenoir City is a city in Loudon County, in the state's eastern region, southwest of Knoxville along the Tennessee River. Town Creek Road runs near the high school close to Lenoir City. A baby had been murdered there a few months after its despondent mother who had lost her husband in a car wreck. The woman slipped into insanity and the baby was to pay for it. If you drive late at night along Town Creek Road near the intersection with Myers Road, where some rocks jut out, do not be surprised if you hear a baby crying. That poor child is still crying for its murderess mother.

McMINN COUNTY

ATHENS

Athens is a city in McMinn County and the home to haunted Wesleyan College and the once upon a time Two Lovers Trees. Years ago, a British soldier was wounded in a battle and found by the chief of a local tribe who nursed him back to health. The soldier fell in love with the chief's daughter and they were allowed to marry. A jealous rival for the hand of the maiden tricked the soldier into the woods where he killed him. The maiden came upon the scene and when she saw her lover was dead, she killed herself. The chief had them buried together at that spot and planted an acorn and a hackberry seed in their graves. Soon a tall oak and a beautiful hackberry grew there. The Wesleyan College was established at that spot in 1857 but special care was taken not to disturb the Lovers' Trees. After standing for an amazing one hundred and sixty-five years, the two trees died in the 1940's and were removed. A memorial commemorating the two Lovers' Trees now mark the spot. Ever since the college was founded, ghostly figures have been spotted roaming the campus. Disembodied whispers and voices have been heard. The spirits are friendly and are thought to that of the two lovers.

Woodlawn Bed and Breakfast, located at 110 Keith Lane in Athens, is haunted by a nameless ghost. Some believe it is a Union Soldier stationed in the area who passed away for some unknown reason. Though there was no battle fought in the area, there was much disease resulting in death. Who ever it is rocks rocking chairs, slams doors and does other apparently harmless things.

CALHOUN

The "Lady in the Gray Gown" opens the front door and walks up the winding staircase at the Pinhook Plantation House B&B in the town of Calhoun in McMinn County. A spirit know as the Monk and his ghostly friends hold a meeting late some nights in the appropriately named Gathering Room.

ETOWAH

Etowah is a city in McMinn County. Years ago, the Etowah High School was haunted by a senior student who committed suicide on the basketball court when his team lost an important game. He loved basketball so much, it is said that he still played it on that basketball court late at night even though he was dead. When the high school was torn down in the 1990's and replaced by the Etowah City School, he can still be seen wearing an old Etowah High School Basketball jersey and playing basketball in the new basketball court.

ENGLEWOOD

They say that if you go to the football field at Central High School in Englewood, a town in

McMinn County, at night, you can see the phantom people in gothic clothing pointing at you from the corner of the track. Be sure to get permission to go there or you may see police pointing at you.

SWEETWATER

The town of Sweetwater lies both in Monroe and McMinn counties with most of the population in Monroe. The ghost of a Union Soldier from the Civil War is said to live in Lost Sea Cave in the Craighead Caverns in Sweetwater. He was killed while spying on Confederate soldiers. He has an unseen pet, the ghost of a jaguar, a species of large cat, that likes to brush its tail against visitors.

MARION COUNTY

JASPER

Jasper is a town in and is the county seat of Marion County. Years ago, a man killed the woman he was having an affair with, stuffed her in a sack and threw her off the East Valley Bridge. She obviously was not happy with that as she will rise up out of the river and swoop down on you if you are stupid enough to go to the bridge midnight on Halloween, honk your horn three times, blink the lights three times and then get out the car.

SOUTH PITTSBURGH

The Baumgartner house, built by the first undertaker in the city of South Pittsburgh in Marion County, is directly across the street from a cemetery. I think you know what that means. Three family members are said to haunt the building. A female ghost thought to be the original owner's wife appears wearing a blue dress while a dark haired, good looking male ghost as well as a slender tall man with a short hair cut wearing a long john shirt and slacks are her companions. The three ghostly residents show up in rooms that have not been used for awhile and just recently opened. Have they been waiting in those unused rooms for an audience to show?

SUCK CREEK

Suck Creek is a small community on the edges of Prentice Cooper Wildlife Management area in rural Marion County and not far from the Hamilton County line and Chattanooga. It got its name from a creek running by the community that had whirlpools that sucked objects down. A trail, known as the Cumberland Trail, in the Suck Creek canyons leads up Signal Mountain and is haunted by the phantom of a slave who was killed while trying to escape to freedom. He can be seen and heard groaning as he roams the area seeking revenge against his murderers.

WHITWELL

Whitwell is a city in Marion County. Years ago an explosion at Mines #21 in the Gray's Creek area in the "Pocket" of Whitwell Mountain killed thirteen miners. Even though the mine was sealed up, people have seen the wheat lamps of the miners coming out of the ground and then disappearing. Sounds like ghost lights to me!

MEIGS COUNTY

I have not found any ghost stories for this county as yet. If you know any please email me at jamesfosterrobinson@live.com and I will include it in any future volume or revision. Type GHOST in the subject heading so I will not miss it.

MONROE COUNTY

I have not found any ghost stories for this county as yet. If you know any please email me at jamesfosterrobinson@live.com and I will include it in any future volume or revision. Type GHOST in the subject heading so I will not miss it.

MORGAN COUNTY

RUGBY

The town of Rugby, partly in Morgan County, and partly in Scott County, has a guided tour of the community. It used to be a Victorian attempt at a utopia settlement in the Cumberland Mountains. For more information on the tours go to www.historicrugby.org.

One of the houses in the settlement is said to be haunted by the ghost of a man, a land agent by profession, who passed away while waiting for his son to arrive in Rugby. The Kingstone Lisle Inn is also haunted by two ghosts. One is the mother of the founder of Rugby and the other is known as "the snoring ghost". In addition to his disembodied snoring, he likes to pull the covers back on the beds. The Library with books belonging to the founder and original first editions brought over from England at the town's beginning are still watched over by the ghost of the curator. And his dog is still trying get out the door at night to do his ghostly duty.

The Newbury House Inn was the scene of a murder suicide in Room 13 years ago and apparently their ghosts may still haunt the place. When the Inn burned down, legend says that screams were heard coming from Room 13 as it burned.

A phantom coach still rumbles through the village carrying the ghost of a man who had worked hard in the 1960-70's to restore the town.

SUNBRIGHT

Sunbright is a city in Morgan County. The ghost of girl, who had been killed by her father in the early 1960's, is often seen pacing back and forth on the Burntmill Bridge. She is sometimes seen falling off that bridge into the water without making a splash.

WARTBURG

The small town of Wartburg is not far from Frozen Head State Park in rural Morgan County. Petit Lane runs off of Highway 27 just south of Wartburg's city limits. An evil spirit roams a field off the road in search of victims. Years ago, around the time of the Civil War, a slave on a nearby plantation, fed up with the terrible abuse by the owner, killed the owner's daughter. It is not known what happened to that slave, but it is known that he still wanders the fields where he worked. If you have the courage to go that that field at midnight when the moon is full, you might see his ghost carrying a pitch fork. If you do, I would get right out of there.

WHITE OAK

The Ghost of White Oak lives in a century old house apparently unused for over thirty years in the community of White Oak in Morgan County. The spirit has been seen in the house and outside sometimes riding a cow. That is what I said - riding a cow!

POLK COUNTY

There are a number of ghostly miners still in evidence in the Ducktown and Copperhill area of Polk County. If you are brave enough to venture near long abandoned mine shafts, be careful. You might be startled by the screams of agony of the dead miners. Some say that you can even see their wispy forms floating about those old mine shaft entrances.

RHEA COUNTY

GRAYSVILLE

An overhanging rock on Graysville Mountain just outside Graysville, a town in Rhea County, is haunted by several unspecified ghosts. Some of those who have visited the rock claimed to have been overwhelmed by feelings of suicide.

ROANE COUNTY

HARIMAN CITY

Harriman City lies primarily in Roane County, with a small extension into Morgan County. Swan Pond Baptist Church is apparently haunted by a preacher who hung himself a couple of decades ago. His ghost has been spotted hanging in the bell tower around midnight. Strange noises have been heard coming from the church when it is supposed to be empty. Red or green lights in the shape of eyes have also been observed at night. Local legend claims that if you drive three circles around the church at a specific time on a certain Saturday of the month, everything will disappear around you for a few seconds. The church is now apparently used only on Sundays for services.

In 1994, after over one hundred years of being dry, the town of Harriman voted to go wet and allow the sale of alcohol. Over the years, the Temperance building, now used as the City Hall, had been the headquarters for the fight against the "demon rum". A number of ghosts, including those of city councilmen and Civil War Soldiers, are said to haunted the premises. They have been seen peeking out of the windows at night and walking around inside.

Cornstalk Heights in Harriman has over one

hundred and fifty historical homes. One home is haunted by a young lady wearing victorian style clothing. Other houses are populated by ghosts in 1890's style garb.

KINGSTON

Kingston is a city in and the county seat of Roane County, Tennessee, and is adjacent to Watts Bar Lake. Fort Southwest Point is an historical site in Kingston. Visitors to the fort have reported feeling an unseen presence and what heard they thought were sounds from the past. Unexplained gun shots have also been heard.

ROCKWOOD

A ghost used to haunt Rockwood, a small town, in Roane County, years ago and may still do so even though the house has been torn down. A man died supposedly of a heart attack and began to haunt his house. He kept changing things in the pictures on the wall; flowers would be out of position for example. Disembodied footsteps were heard at night and a white specter would float around in the air. Then there are the screams of children killed in a fire at an old school house in Rockwood that can still be heard coming from the ruins - that is, if the ruins still exist.

WHEAT

The community of Wheat, originally known as Bald Hill, was located in the Roane County section of present day Oak Ridge. It was a going concern until it gave way to the Manhattan Project and its secret city. The George Jones Memorial Baptist Church and its cemetery became isolated and remains that way today. Since at least the 1970's, the place is said to be haunted by an evil spirit that roams the area after dark. They also say that it might be the ghost of man who was murdered and buried there and who is looking for revenge.

SCOTT COUNTY

A psychiatric patient named Cora at the Scott County Hospital killed herself by diving off the end of her bed. They say that she still goes up in the elevator to the floor where the nursery is to see the newborn babies. She also likes to open doors and knock things off shelves.

SEQUATCHIE COUNTY

MARION

Grayson Manor in Marion is haunted by the ghost of General Grayson, a doctor during the Civil War, who apparently went crazy and stabbed his wife and his children to death. His disembodied footsteps can be heard downstairs coming from the bedroom overhead where he had hung himself. You may even heard a loud thud and a creaking sound that they say is the Doctor hanging himself again and again and again.

SEVIER COUNTY

GATLINBERG

Gatlinburg, a mountain resort city in Sevier County, is known for more that Dollyworld. It is also haunted. A young woman had committed suicide in the Greenbrier Restaurant and sometimes puts in a ghostly appearance. The Holiday Inn Sunspree Resort has a number of ghostly guests. A business man, who shot himself in Room 471, apparently hangs around the pool in the form of a shadow. Back in the 1980's, a group of Boy Scouts stayed on the 7th floor. Their leader, it is said, went crazy and killed a number of the boys before being caught. Now the disembodied sound of running and screaming can occasionally be heard on that floor.

Room 413 in the Holiday Inn Sunspree Resort is said to be haunted by two young girls murdered by a man who they picked up at a local bar and brought back to their room. Noises have been heard coming from the empty bathroom and objects in the room move by themselves from one place to another.

In a certain room at 3:33 AM in the Mount LeCounte, a little girl is said to appear by the bed and watch the occupants sleeping. Do not ask me how the sleeping people know she is there.

Over fifteen years ago, two employees of the Rocky Top Inn were killed in the old office at the back of the building. Their killer was caught and executed. They say that you can hear the victims' screams and some people have reported seeing their specters by the fountain and in the back parking lot.

There is or was a site called the Mystery Mansion in the heart of Gatlinburg. Some years ago, a little girl fell to her death off a balconey at that hotel one one near it. Now, two weeks before the yearly anniversary of her death, her ghost appears, starts to cry and points up to the balcony she fell from.

PIGEON fORGE

The Family Inn by the Dixie Stampede in Pigeon Forge, a mountain resort city in Sevier County, is said to be haunted by an old lady who, while working late one night, was murdered. Now, on the same day of her untimely demise, you can see her shadow watching you.

SEVIERVILLE

Servierville is a city in and the county seat of Sevier County. Ghosts and disembodied voices occur at the Bluff Mountain old hotel site. People have also reported a feeling of dread at that spot. The phenomena may be linked to an old cemetery a couple of hundred feet off a nearby trail. The graveyard is said to date back to the 1790's when a small military post was attacked and every soldier killed by a band of rogue Indians.

The Old Eledge House is said to be haunted by Mr. Eledge who died of a heart attack in the house. The disembodied sounds of Mr. Eledge and his children laughing can be heard throughout the house and the lights flicker off and on.

SULLIVAN COUNTY

BLOOMINGDALE

Bloomingdale is in Sullivan County, near Kingsport. A witch is said to be buried on a hill top in an cemetery on the Timbertree Road in Bloomingdale. Visitors to the graveyard say they can hear the witch beating on her coffin cover, apparently still wanting out.

BLOUNTVILLE

The Sullivan County News used to be published in a building in Blountville, a community in Sullivan County. A ghost named "George" haunted this building. No one knows who he is or was and why he haunted the place. Starting in the 1940's, he made his presence known by opening and closing doors during working hours. An apparition wearing a gray suit is often spotted entering the back door. One editor apparently had enough of this disturbing visitor and fired a shot at George. You can guess the outcome.

BRISTOL

The city of Bristol lies in Sullivan County, in northeast Tennessee. A disgruntled ghost makes it presences known in the Arnett Home. It walks around the place both day and night and whispers faintly to people alone in the house. Gun shots from unknown and unseen sources have been heard in the backyard.

Local legend says that a janitor raped and killed a young girl many years ago and left her body in the salad bar in the cafeteria of Sullivan East High School. Now it is claimed that you can hear screams in a low deep voice coming from that salad bar.

Tennessee High School is thought to have at least three ghosts. "Agnes" is the most well known and supposedly drown in the swimming pool on Graduation Night many years ago. Her ghost has been seen walking at night in the old section of the school. Next is the ghost of a student, a very good athlete who was killed by a car one night while walking home. His ghost hangs out around the school's field house. The most bizarre ghost is that of a phantom train like an old steam engine that appears in the auditorium, races down the hall and disappears in the old gym. This ghost maybe related to an old railway they say used to run through that spot. All this ghostly activity must make this school an interesting place to attend.

There is supposedly a haunted hollow in Chinqapin Grove at Bristol. People have reported the feeling of being watched while traveling down the small road there. They have also said that time and space somehow seems screwed up from time to time. I will not comment on what they had before driving down that road.

Weaver Cemetery lies just outside of Bristol and is one of the oldest graveyards in Tennessee. There have been reports of an occasional ghost and the odd feeling of unseen presences. Then there is the "Black Aggie", a hooded figure that comes out at night and roams among the tombstones.

KINGSPORT

Kingsport is a city in Sullivan County with small portions in Hawkins County. A young girl died of a heart attack at Ketron Middle School. Now she is spotted some nights wearing a long white dress and wandering the hall and in the gym.

In 1922, a man named Hugh Hamblen was killed by a car one night on the Netherland Inn Road. On foggy nights, Hugh in a trench coat is often seen warning people with his outstretched hands to slow down in the fog.

They say that a young woman who lived in Rotherwood Mansion had bad luck with husbands. Her newly wed always seemed to die for various reasons shortly after the wedding. She became desponded and drowned herself in the nearby Holston River. This unfortunate lady is still seen on foggy nights wearing her wedding dress and crying while standing in her room's window of the mansion. She has also been spotted in her wedding dress rushing down to the Holston River.

The Rotherwood Mansion was once owned by Joshua Phipps who brutally treated his slaves. Then one day he fell sick and, as he lay on his bed, his mouth and nose suddenly filled with flies and he suffocated. At his funeral, they had trouble getting the casket up the hill to the graveyard. It seemed to become very heavy and a number of horses were required to drag it up to the grave site. Then the skies went dark and a big black dog jumped out of the coffin and raced down the hill. The clouds burst and rain fell. They quickly buried the casket and went home. That is what local legend says.

That black dog became known as the "Hound of Hell" and is said to roam the land around the mansion. If you are out there on dark and stormy nights, you just might hear its low, mournful howl. As for the mansion, people claim that when it rains blood stains from the punished slaves appear on the mansion's floors.

Wait! I am not finished! The ghosts of Joshua Phipps and his mistress who also mistreated the slaves apparently haunt the mansion itself. Wait! I thought that the "Hound of Hell" was the evil spirit of Phipps! Anyhow, his mistress, a slave herself, was killed by the slaves she brutalized. Meanwhile, Phipps likes to pull the covers off sleepers while laughing an evil, sadistic laugh.

A Mr. Sensabaugh is said to have killed his entire family years ago in the stream which runs through the tunnel named after him. Orbs of light and strange figures are seen in that tunnel and a baby's crying can be heard. Reports have it that there are two tunnels, one with the road through it and the other has the stream. The outline of a woman has often appeared in the back seat of cars going through the tunnel with the road.

The four mile long Long Island lies in the Holston River at Kingsport. It is cursed. For many years, the island was sacred to the native Americans in the area who cursed it as unusable for the white settlers. Anyone going on the island is liable to become violent and very distressed. In the 1940's, a young man was caught dallying with his girl friend by his father and both were killed when the father became really upset and violent. Now the ghost of the insane father is doomed to walk the island at night looking for more victims. The spirits of long dead Native Americans are also said to to walk that island. Ghostly canoes have been spotted on the river and strange noises heard. That is one curse I suggest you leave well enough alone.

UNICOI COUNTY

ERWIN

Jobe Cemetery is on Main Street in Erwin in Unicoi County. The ghost of a mean hobo named "Old Dawg", who died about one hundred years ago, hangs out in that cemetery apparently scaring anyone who dares to enter it.

The Nolichucky River which flows through Unicoi County is haunted by the ghosts of people who drown there and by evil spirits that hide in the cracks and crevices of the area known as the Devil's Looking Glass, a sheer cliff on one shore. They say that the spirits of Daniel Boone and John Sevier as well as screaming banshees have been seen on the river. Flora, a woman who drown in the river during the Great Depression, still walks the river banks after dark.

An area of the river known as Bumpass Cove has shadowy figures moving around after dark and the disembodied sounds of thundering hooves can be heard.

Bumpass Cove Graveyard sits on a tall hill off Bumpass Cove Road. This cemetery is apparently circular and the road goes around it in a circle. It is said that a jeep with a couple in it rolled off a hill by the graveyard into the river when it got accidentally knocked out gear. Both people drowned. Local legend now says that if you drive around the graveyard three times at midnight under a full moon, the outline of that jeep's headlights will appear and chase you. Why? I do not know!

In the 1920's, a phantom horse was seen wandering around the railroad tracks near the National Fish Hatchery in Erwin and nearby woods at night. Apparently it is still seen today.

UNION COUNTY

MAYNARDVILLE

The Union County court house in Maynardville is home to the ghost of a man who was sentenced to death and executed many years ago. He keeps opening the doors like he is trying to get out.

For some unknown reason, several female ghosts haunt Horace Maynard Middle School. Their specters have been seen running down the halls at night by the janitors. Their disembodied laughter often rings out and they liked to knock at the front door. Of course, there is no one there when people check.

WASHINGTON COUNTY

JOHNSON CITY

Johnson City is a city in Carter, Sullivan, and Washington counties with most of the city being in Washington County. It may well be the most haunted city in the state. The East Tennessee State University has a number of ghosts attending the campus. A female teacher, who supposedly killed herself, is said to haunt Burleson Hall. Many believe her ghost has possessed a portrait of her father hanging in the building. The eyes of Mr. Burleson seem to follow you around. Sidney Gilbreath, who started this campus years ago, haunts Gilbreath Hall which is named after him. He will shut open doors and windows when a thunderstorm approaches.

John Gilbreath was the first president of East Tennessee State University in 1911, and was very strict. His ghost walks the halls of Gilbreath Hall after dark making sure his original rules are still enforced.

The elevator in Lucille Clement Hall, the Women's Residence, is said to be haunted by "Marble Boy", the ghost of a young boy who died in that elevator. He also has been heard dropping marbles on the ceilings of every room in the hall.

When students yell at him to stop, it sounds like he dumps all his marbles at once. Marble Boy also likes to change the channel on the TV and even turn it off. He also delights in turning on water faucets.

A librarian who liked her job so much that she helped out after retiring. Then she died of a heart attack in the stacks. Apparently she still puts books back in their right spot when they are left lying around by students. Many students feel that they are being watched by an unseen presence. One of the staff saw her once down in the stacks and refused to go back down there.

The ghost called Alice is also known as the Screaming Ghost. She was supposedly the daughter of a wealthy business man, George Carter. When her parents refused to allow her to marry the young man she loved, she committed suicide with poison. She now haunts Cooper Hall, or so they say.

Yoakley Hall, once a women's dorm, but now an office building, is haunted by a former female student who killed herself by jumping out of a window on the top floor. Soon after this tragedy, students and faculty began to see a mysterious figure jumping out or just leaning out of a window on the third floor. Many female students became depressed in the hall and it was subsequently turned into an office building.

The Okolona road exit is another one of those haunted magnetic hills you hear about from time to time. The story goes that if you stop on the exit, put your car in neutral, it will start rolling up the incline. The local explanation says that your car is being pushed by the ghosts of two people killed when their car stalled on the exit and was hit by another car. They say that you can sometimes see the imprints of their hands on car's back windows. They do not want you to suffer their fate. One good way to make sure you do not, is to NOT STOP on that exit.

Swingle Hospital, the first hospital in Johnson City and located near Science Hill High School and Heritage Manor, is said to be haunted by patients of Dr. Swingle who died on his operating table back in the 1920's. The disembodied voices of the doctor and his staff supposedly can be heard near the front entrance while the screams of the dead patients can be heard at the back of the building. The place is apparently closed up and the doors and windows boarded up. It is not a good idea to trespass on the property

Mathes Music Hall abounds with cold spots. Disembodied voices and footsteps are also heard

A mischievous spirit at the Sigma Fraternity House on ETSU campus likes to rearrange things and walk around snapping his fingers to a beat only he hears.

The John Sevier Center, a retirement home in Johnson City, is in a building that once was a hotel, a dance club and a brothel. In December of 1989, a terrible fire broke out in the home and sixteen people died of smoke inhalation. Local TV News showed footage of elderly people and staff on the top floors waving for help. Not long after this tragedy, ghostly figures were seen waving from windows and apparitions moved around the halls and rooms. Some visitors reported feeling unseen presences in the building.

JONESBOROUGH

Jonesborough, a town in and the county seat of Washington County, is Tennessee's oldest and most mysterious town. Founded 1780, it was the capital of the ill-fated State of Franklin and General and the future President Andrew Jackson made his home there at that time. For years, people have seen the ghost of Jackson walking around the main street, amazingly almost every time in daylight. Interestingly enough, only people on the opposite side of the street see him while those on the same side do not. Jackson also like to hang around the Christopher Taylor House even after it was moved to a new location.

John Sevier, the Governor of the State of Franklin as well as Tennessee's first Governor, has been seen haunting a house in the area. And do not forget the mysterious Goblin that is said to live in a woods outside Jonesborough.

IMAGES OF TENNESSEE

As far as I can determine the following images are in the public domain. If any of these images belong to you, and you wish them removed please email me at jamesfosterrobinson@live.com with the details. As the writer and the publisher via createspace.com, I am able to make changes "on the fly" so to speak.

Bell Witch House

John Bell

Historical Marker Bell Witch

Artist Sketch of Betsy Bell

Andrew Jackson is said to haunt the Hermitage.

Some have claimed to have seen the ghost of Elvis Presley
at his home, "Graceland"

The State Capitol building is said to be haunted by
both the original architect, William Strickland and
Samuel Morgan who oversaw the construction of
the building.

MIDDLE TENNESSEE

Middle Tennessee is that part of the state that lies east of of the western crossing of the Tennessee River and west of the line where the Eastern Time zone changes into the Central time zone. However, Hardin County, located on the both sides of the Tennessee River, is considered part of West Tennessee while Bledsoe County, Cumberland and Marion counties, despite being in the Central Time Zone, are said to be in East Tennessee.

COUNTIES

BEDFORD COUNTY

SHELBYVILLE

Shelbyville is a city and county seat in

Bedford County. Apparitions of some kind and the usual cold spots occur in Hillcrest Cemetery. Sorry folks. That is all I know about Hillcrest Crest Cemetery.

A very friendly ghost named Aunt Crecy used to reside at 610 North Jefferson Street in the historical district of Shelbyville. She was Lucretia Pearson, who had lived in the house until she died around 1892. Lucretia was known for her good-natured, friendly, and courteous personality. She loved her house so much that apparently she did leave it even in death. Visitors to the house in later years claimed to feel a gentle presence. Aunt Crecy helped out around the house by doing such things as closing open windows when a storm was approaching. She had also put in appearances sometimes. When a fire in 1931 destroyed her bedroom, she was never seen again.

WARTRACE

The Walking Horse Inn in Wartrace has thirteen rooms and was once used to repatriate Civil War prisoners, several who passed away there waiting release. In the 1970's, four guests were shot and killed by a distressed Vietnam War veteran having a flashback. Now people have heard disembodied voices, gunshots and the sound of running feet late at night. Room 11 apparently has an eerie atmosphere and visitors have reported that they were being watched by someone unseen.

CANNON COUNTY

I have not found any ghost stories for this county as yet. If you know any please email me at jamesfosterrobinson@live.com and I will include it in any future volume or revision. Type GHOST in the subject heading so I will not miss it.

CHEATHAM COUNTY

I have not found any ghost stories for this county as yet. If you know any please email me at jamesfosterrobinson@live.com and I will include it in any future volume or revision. Type GHOST in the subject heading so I will not miss it.

CLAY COUNTY

I have not found any ghost stories for this county as yet. If you know any please email me at jamesfosterrobinson@live.com and I will include it in any future volume or revision. Type GHOST in the subject heading so I will not miss it.

COFFEE COUNTY

MANCHESTER

Manchester is a city in and the county seat of Coffee County. The historic Tower House Inn, aka the Tower House, was built years ago by John P. Adams. About this time, his wife, May, and their little son, Marion, died. Mr. Adams himself passed away around 1943, I believe. In 1963, May has been seen weeping and John often strolls from the men's parlor to the front room. Even little Marion, a blonde haired boy clothed in a soft light, is often spied in the boy's room upstairs. Ghost tours and house tours are available. Contact the owners, Dan and Carol Gist of the GhostLabs Research Society. More information on the hauntings can be found at Ghostlabs.com.

Martin Clement Hall is the oldest building at the University of Tennessee campus in Manchester. They say that a female student, who committed suicide on the fourth floor, haunts the place. Around Halloween, a Haunted House is staged there but not on the fourth floor. Perhaps it is thought to be scary enough up there.

TULLAHOMA

The Concord Cemetery is haunted by the

ghost of Sadie Baker, one of Coffee County's oldest known ghosts. Nothing is known about her except that her name appears by itself on a simple gravestone. Some speculate that she used to be a witch, others that she died as a small child. She could be one of two apparitions seen in the cemetery or she could be both. One is that of a child playing among the stones while the other is an adult woman wandering the graveyard at night.

Apparitions were seen by night shift workers in the old Walmart building in what I believe is now the Forest Gallery Shopping Center in Tullahoma. They also reported that someone unseen would tap them on their shoulders or pinched their behinds. Merchandise moved by itself off pallets; items disappeared and shelves fell down. Strange music could be heard when nothing was playing. Ghostly visages appeared in the security balls hanging from the ceiling. Add to the scary mix the sounds of screams and mysterious voices coming over the PA system. It is not known if the phenomena continued in the new store that replaced Walmart after it moved.

There is an old burnt down orphanage near a lake at Tullahoma where disembodied cries for help can be heard. The pleas are thought to be of children burnt to death or drowned in the lake.

DAVIDSON COUNTY

ANTIOCH

They say that if you live on Loroe Lane in Antioch, a community in southeastern Davidson County, an old lady, who was killed by a coyote in the woods off the lane, will watch you sleep at night. She has also been known to follow young kids around after dark. This lady is known as the Antioch Deathkiller. Why? I do not know. I have not heard of her hurting anyone. Maybe she is scarier than the Boogy Man and helps to keep the kids home at night.

NASHVILLE

Nashville is the capital of Tennessee and the county seat of Davidson County. It is located on the Cumberland River in the north-central part of the state. The Belmont Mansion built by Adelicia Hayes in 1849 is haunted. Security guards, because they work at night, are more likely to see ghost phenomena. The guards at the university have reported seeing Adelicia floating around the mansion. She even sets off the motion detectors occasionally.

The Capitol Records Building in Nashville was built on the site of an old mansion belonging to a Jacob Schnell and then to his two daughters after he died. Employees of Capitol Records reported seeing the apparitions of the two daughters walking the halls, locking doors, moving things around and fooling with the equipment.

In 1987, a visitor staying in the Congress Inn, complained of someone unseen lying on his legs and not letting him roll over. The staff advised the visitor it might have to do with the fact that the motel office was a hospital in the Civil War and the dead were buried in the walls of the basement. Anyone want to test that theory out?

The old Donelson Hospital, one of the oldest Nashville hospitals, was closed down years ago, but apparently is used for storage for current hospitals and doctor's offices. The place is haunted. Day or night, screams and moans can be heard as well as footsteps and clanging on the walls. The old psych ward reportedly has a strong sense of energy and is extremely chilly even in summer. By the way, there is no air conditioning working in the old building

The Hawkins House on Ninth Street in Nashville was home to a poltergeist for some time in the 1960's. There occurred the "classic poltergeist" activities such as footsteps and banging noises. The word, Poltergeist, is German for "noisy spirit".

One of America's most famous presidents was Andrew Jackson. Jackson's old home, the Hermitage, in Nashville is also haunted. Some years ago, something or someone sometimes threw pots and pans around the kitchen at night. Then there was the eerie sound of a chain being pulled across the front porch and those of a horse being rode up and down the stairs. Recently the specters of his long passed away slaves have been seen on the mansion's front balcony at Jefferson's bedroom window and disembodied voices heard.

Madison is a neighborhood in northeast Nashville. The now closed Duff's Smorgasbord was thought to be haunted. Late at night, the disembodied laughter of a woman could be heard as well as the crash of pots or stock to the floor. Apparently nothing was found amis when employees checked.

The Market Street Pub and Brewery in downtown Nashville is currently or was a restaurant and bar. The establishment was possibly haunted as chairs moved around the floor all by themselves. Light fixtures swung without any evidence of a draft. Lights would go off by themselves but would turn back on when a human demand it. When alone in the place, many people felt an eerie presence.

Nashville' s Opryland is still graced by the ghostly presence of Hank Williams, the famous Country Western singer. When one singer was practicing a Hank Williams song, the lights went out in the middle of the rendition. Maybe Hank disapproved of that singer's version of his music. Another ghost is a woman wearing a blue and white checked gingham dress and believed to be the ghost of Patsy Cline.

The ghost of a lady named Mrs. McGavock, wanders the corridors of the Opryland Hotel at night. Staff have seen her in the wee hours after midnight.

The Two Rivers Mansion and Golf Course has been the scene of ghostly people walking in the mansion and disembodied footsteps following visitors around. Items inexplicably disappear. Lights turn off and on by themselves. Many visitors have the eerie feeling of being watched by unseen eyes. The site used to be an Indian burial ground. An old man used to live in the house that was there before the golf course was built. They say that he buried his money in jars in the ground. Local legend claims that if you go to the spot where the house used to be, you just might hear him opening his jars. Do not bother to look for those jars. They were found when that old house was torn down.

The Wilowen House is apparently home to a

poltergeist, an evil abusive entity who does not like anyone living there for any length of time. Local legend says that it is a disgruntled old man that wants to be left alone and will go to ghostly lengths to get his way.

A certain house known to be haunted on Cedar Lane right across from Sunnyside Mansion in Sevier Park was a hospital in the Civil War. One resident spied an unknown girl enter a bedroom but was not there when he checked that bedroom. She was described as having blonde hair and dressed in 1970's style of clothing. That same resident had an inordinate number of flies buzzing around a lamp in his room and sprayed them. When the dust settled, that was nary a dead fly to be found.

A few years ago, an assistant manager working alone late one night in a movie theater in Nashville saw a figure, dressed completely in white, standing at the front of the auditorium who vanished quickly when he looked away for a second and then back again. When he started to go down the stairs, a large pole fan crashed loudly down to the floor directly behind him.

The State Capitol building is said to be haunted by both the original architect, William Strickland and Samuel Morgan who oversaw the construction of the building. These two men feuded for nine years over the budget and costs. Strickland died in 1854 and was buried in a newly constructed vault on the north side. Legend says that their feud still continues. Police have responded to complaints of noises and found nothing. But they could hear disembodied voices arguing.

The old Union Station is today a hotel in Nashville. There was a train wreck nearby on July 9th in 1819 killing and injuring over two hundred people. Of course, the place is haunted. Loud banging on walls and doors awaken guests at night and there is temporary interruptions of power to television sets and the lights, especially on the 5th and 6th floors.

Mount Olivet Cemetery at 1101 Lebanon Pike has many prominent people from early Nashville history buried there. The graveyard is haunted. The classic "Black Aggie," a dark specter, walks around the place after dark. Strange lights have been seen moving around, and orbs mysteriously appear in film after it's been developed.

The Ryman Auditorium, located in downtown Nashville, was named after Captain Tom Ryman, who now haunts the place. He is very mischievous and likes turning off the lights.

Saint Mary's Catholic Church, founded in 1847, is allegedly home to some ghosts. One phantom, who roams the church, was first seen in the 1930's. In 1937, the Monsignor was awaken by a furious pounding on the door several times but never found out who or what was doing it. Three different stories explain the ghost. The first says it is a priest who died during the church's construction. The second one claims that it is the ghost of a Chaplain who served in the Confederate Army during the Civil War. When he was severely wounded, they took him to the church where he died and is still hanging around. The favorite version says it is the spirit of Bishop Richard Pius Miles, the first bishop of the Diocese of Nashville, who passed away in 1860 and was buried in the church basement. The ghostly activity seems to have stop when his remains were discovered in 1969.

DEKALB COUNTY

DRY CREEK

If you venture out after dark in Dry Creek, something unknown and unseen will walk up behind you. It will chase you if you run. If you do run and then stop, the unknown presence behind you will also stop. Some people claimed to have had a look at it and that it look human but had no face. Gruesome!

DICKSON COUNTY

WHITE BLUFF

The White Screamer haunts White Bluff in Middle Tennessee in Dickson County. No one knows who or what it is but it has been blamed for the massacre of a family years ago. The father of the family hearing this terrible screaming out in the woods and went out to investigate it but never found out what caused it. As he was returning home, he heard screaming coming from his farmhouse. When he got there, he found his whole family torn to shreds as if by a wild animal. Was it a raving ghost, a mountain lion or Bigfoot? Locals say the White Screamer is a misty apparition that leaves burnt patches of grass wherever it has been.

FENTRESS COUNTY

I have not found any ghost stories for this county as yet. If you know any please email me at jamesfosterrobinson@live.com and I will include it in any future volume or revision. Type GHOST in the subject heading so I will not miss it.

FRANKLIN COUNTY

COWAN

At night the tombstones shine in Cowan Cemetery, in the city of Cowan in Franklin County. The apparitions of people had also been spotted standing by these shining gravestones. The Franklin Pearson House is said to be a hot bed of paranormal activity mostly harmless.

DECHERD

North Junior High School in Decherd is haunted by the spirit of a girl who calls out people's names in a pleading voice, asking for help in the afternoon and early evening. When they turn to see who it is, there is no one there.

MONTEAGLE

Monteagle is a town in Franklin, Grundy, and Marion counties in the Cumberland Plateau region. An apartment in the Fairmont Apartments is said to be haunted but no one knows by whom or what. Disembodied footsteps have been heard at all hours. Covers have been pulled off of people's beds in the middle of the night. Residents have heard their names called out at night like "the wind blowing". Once a living room got very cold and footprints appeared on the carpet. But no one was seen making them.

SEWANNEE

The Dubose Conference Center in th town of Sewanee is haunted by two ghosts. One is that of Sidney, a young lady who hung herself in a closet in the last room in the East Hall. Many people who have stayed in that room say they had felt her ghostly presence. The previous caretaker, Dr. Dubose, liked his job so much that he hangs around the grounds long after he passed away.

The small college of The University of the South sits atop Monteagle Mountain in Sewanee. A headless gownsman apparently appears in the campus's library during Homecoming Week or finals periods on certain years. It might be a long dead student still trying to graduate.

Tuckaway Dormitory was an inn before becoming a dormitory. The ghost of a hunter, who had been killed in a hunting accident after staying at the inn, like it so much that he chose it as his favorite spot to haunt. The phantom hunter appears before the last student who goes to bed and apparently grabs his throat and ties to choke him. Also three students, who lived in a room on the third floor of Tuckaway Hall, committed suicide and now like to stir things up. Many student do not want to be assigned to that room because of their ghostly shenanigans.

At Walsh-Ellet Hall, disembodied footsteps are heard come up the staircase and into the corridor pausing by an open door. A chill descends and then the footsteps continue down the hall and down the staircase on the other side. Two enclosed staircases are the exterior of Walsh-Ellet Building. One is labeled 'UP' and the other is labeled 'Down'. A ghostly gownsman, this one with a head, is often seen on those stairs, especially is the human student is going the wrong way on the labeled stairs. His shadowy figure wears the traditional robe of the Order of the Gownsman. Sometimes just his head is seen floating around! There are two different tales of who he was. In one version he was a student who loved the college so much that after he was decapitated in a car accident on a winding road up to the college he continues to attend it. The other, possibly a silly tale, states that a seminary student spend all his time filling his head with so much knowledge that it became so heavy, it fell off! Right! I think the first story is more likely.

GILES COUNTY

ELKTON

Hanniwal Bridge, abandoned in the 19th Century, spans the Elk River at Elkton, a city in

Giles County. A mother and her child were killed one night crossing the bridge when their carriage suddenly flipped over into the river. If you go to that bridge late at night, you just might hear the mother's screams and the faint cries of the baby.

GRUNDY COUNTY

I have not found any ghost stories for this county as yet. If you know any please email me at jamesfosterrobinson@live.com and I will include it in any future volume or revision. Type GHOST in the subject heading so I will not miss it.

HICKMAN COUNTY

I have not found any ghost stories for this county as yet. If you know any please email me at jamesfosterrobinson@live.com and I will include it in any future volume or revision. Type GHOST in the subject heading so I will not miss it.

HOUSTON COUNTY

I have not found any ghost stories for this county as yet. If you know any please email me at jamesfosterrobinson@live.com and I will include it in any future volume or revision. Type GHOST in the subject heading so I will not miss it.

HUMPHREY COUNTY

HURRICANE MILLS

Hurricane Mills is a small community in Humphreys County and centered on Loretta Lynn's Ranch. Loretta Lynn's estate was the scene of a Civil War battle. Apparitions have been seen standing by a bed. Doors are opened and closed by unseen hands. The disembodied sounds of footsteps and chains being dragged across the porch have startled visitors to the place. The home was featured on a Travel Channel special called "Loretta Lynn's Haunted Plantation".

JACKSON COUNTY

I have not found any ghost stories for this county as yet. If you know any please email me at jamesfosterrobinson@live.com and I will include it in any future volume or revision. Type GHOST in the subject heading so I will not miss it.

LAWRENCE COUNTY

I have not found any ghost stories for this county as yet. If you know any please email me at jamesfosterrobinson@live.com and I will include it in any future volume or revision. Type GHOST in the subject heading so I will not miss it.

LEWIS COUNTY

I have not found any ghost stories for this county as yet. If you know any please email me at jamesfosterrobinson@live.com and I will include it in any future volume or revision. Type GHOST in the subject heading so I will not miss it.

LINCOLN COUNTY

FLINTVILLE

The Flintville Ghost Light has been seen for many years off the Flintville Road at a school where railway tracks used to run. Observers say it looks just like a lantern being carrying across the school yard. The mysterious light seems to approach people but disappears when it gets too close. Of course, the light is said to be the ghost of a local resident who was killed by a speeding train.

Like most ghost light there is, at present, no scientific explanation.

KELSO

Golden Hollow Road is in or near Kelso, a community in Lincoln County. In the 1950's, one spring, seven people were killed in a two car collison on the road. Now their ghostly figures are often seen walking about there on warm spring evenings. All seem to be injured but when approached they up and disappear.

MACON COUNTY

I have not found any ghost stories for this county as yet. If you know any please email me at jamesfosterrobinson@live.com and I will include it in any future volume or revision. Type GHOST in the subject heading so I will not miss it.

MARSHAL COUNTY

CHAPEL HILL

Another famous ghost light is the Chapel Hill light that appears at a railway Crossing at Chapel Hill, a town in the northeastern part of Marshall County. Again the light appears to be a lantern that someone unseen is swinging. Again, a railway worker was decapitated by a train many years ago and he is, by lantern light, looking for his lost head. "Phantom trains" have also been reported roaring up and down the tracks at night. Be aware that the police may not allow you to park there anymore. Check with them first before venturing out to the site.

LEWISBURG

The town of Lewisburg is the county seat of Marshall County. There are several legends connected with the Bethbirei Church just outside of Lewisburg. They say that if you steal a bible from that church, you will die! It is claimed that some people who did the dirty deed died that same night! Co-incidence? I wonder? You have been warned. An old cemetery, with graves dating from the early 1800s, surrounds the church. Mysterious lights hover in the cemetery at night while grave stones glow with an eerie green light. There is a feeling of uneasiness about the place. The church itself is haunted by strange figures and lights seen in the windows after dark. Even more disturbing are reports of huge, manlike beasts walking around the area on their hind legs!

\

MAURY COUNTY

COLUMBIA

The community of Columbia is the county seat of Maury County. The abandoned Bear Creek Church in Columbia is unusual. It has two stories, but only the first is accessible. All the windows are painted a red color. Many people believe that the place is guarded by pure evil and mention pictures taken of specters as evidence. There is an abandon cemetery over one hundred years old deep in the woods near Columbia. If you walk past that graveyard, you may hear the sounds like that of someone being murdered and that of children playing.

MONTGOMERY COUNTY

CLARKSVILLE

There was an old building on Amanda Drive from the 1800's, now torn down, in Clarksville, a city in and the county seat of Montgomery County, where eerie, disembodied groaning and moaning as well as the sound of a woman in pleasure could be heard between 11:00 PM and 12:00 AM every other day. The noise is thought to be from the ghost of a prostitute who ran her business from the building and loved her job so much that she is still enjoying in a ghostly form to this day. Sometimes the phantom of a young woman would put in an appearance. Maybe it is the phantom of the hooker looking for more ghostly customers.

Austin Peay State University has a number of haunts. Long past away Governor Austin Peay walks the campus named after him keeping a ghostly eye on university goings-on. The Trahern Theater is one of the places also effected. In 2002 on one afternoon, the theater department was producing a show when the lights dimmed two or three times for no discernable power problem. The stage and third floor is supposedly haunted by a young woman by the name of "Margaret". She likes to fool with the elevators, lock doors, bang on lockers and calling out the name of anyone foolish to be alone in the building at night.

A ghost with no legs was seen floating past an opened door into a hallway on the first floor of Gateway Hospital one night in Clarksville.

An old house behind Reasthaven Cemetery on Highway 41A in Clarksvlle is haunted by a slave who was killed by his master when the slave raped the owner's daughter and made her pregnant. She apparently lost the child before it was born. The ghost of the slave haunts the house and the cemetery apparently in the form of a blue/green light.

A Cumberland riverboat captain, a Mr. Smith, and his wife used to live in the Trahern Mansion which overlooked the Cumberland River in Clarksburg. Mrs. Smith used to sit on the mansion balcony waiting for sight of her husband's safe return. The Captain died of illness while on a trip and his body was lost in an accident on the Mississippi River but, they say, Mrs. Smith still waits in vigil for her husband's safe return.

The Strip is a long line of restaurants and businesses off Interstate 24 in Clarksville. Years ago, it was just farm land and every farm had its own burial plot. When the region was developed, not all the plots were relocated. Some locals feel that those still buried there are a bit perturbed about the situation. One unnamed restaurant is the scene of strange happenings. Disembodied voices and mysterious scratching noises can be heard under the restaurant's floor. Are the deceased hungry and want to come to dinner?

MILLIGAN

Milligan, just outside of Clarksville, is a city in and is the county seat of Montgomery County. A little used road there goes by a Civil War battlefield where you may experience a ghost of a different kind. At a certain spot on the road you can see and hear a river crossing the road. There is no bridge crossing that river for it is not real. It is a ghost river! Get it! If you got our in the middle of that river, they say, you would not get wet but would be perfectly dry.

edited here

PALMYRA

The ghost of E.T. Wickham, a sculptor of statues haunted the head statues he created on the grounds on Buck Smith Road at Palymra just south of Clarksville. He lived in a cabin across the street and strange noises are often heard at the now abandoned building. The statues, in bad condition, were removed a few years ago. There is another ghost story of a man who supposedly killed his ailing wife and, when caught by the son, killed him also. Then the father, in remorse, committed suicide. Now all three of them wander the area in ghostly form. Weird shadows and ghost lights are seen and strange noises heard at night there.

PORT ROYAL

Port Royal is a community on the border of Montgomery and Robertson counties at the confluence of the Red River and Sulphur Fork Creek. It is home to Port Royal State Park and was once a major port on the Red River. The place has a number of ghostly residents. The Masonic Lodge near the Red River has at least two resident specters. One such phantom hangs out upstairs in what was once a doctor's office. It could be heard walking around and moving furniture in an otherwise empty room. Passing motorists notice faces in the upstairs window. Many believe it is the ghost of Willie Woodridge who passed away in the doctor's office in 1903. The second spook is an elderly woman who likes sit on the porch of the building. She is said to be Willie's mother who died when she got the news of Willie's death.

MOORE COUNTY

I have not found any ghost stories for this county as yet. If you know any please email me at jamesfosterrobinson@live.com and I will include it in any future volume or revision. Type GHOST in the subject heading so I will not miss it.

OVERTON COUNTY

HILLHAM

The Old Union Meeting House is of course on Old Union Road in the community of Hilham just outside of Livingston. The building, closed and boarded up for years, is said to be a hotbed of ghostly activity. Strange lights are seen glowing through the cracks in the boarded up windows of the Meeting House. Late at night, passersby have heard beautiful organ music coming from the empty, abandoned church. Many living in the area stay clear of the place.

PERRY COUNTY

I have not found any ghost stories for this county as yet. If you know any please email me at jamesfosterrobinson@live.com and I will include it in any future volume or revision. Type GHOST in the subject heading so I will not miss it.

PICKETT COUNTY

I have not found any ghost stories for this county as yet. If you know any please email me at jamesfosterrobinson@live.com and I will include it in any future volume or revision. Type GHOST in the subject heading so I will not miss it.

PUTMAN COUNTY

COOKVILLE

There is a huge rock on the side of an old dirt road in Cookville, a community Putnam County. Years ago a young woman was killed in an accident at that spot. Then, back in the 1950's, her ghost dressed in white was seen sitting on the rock on the anniversary of her death. Is she still seen?

DRY HOLLOW

Dry Hollow is located in Buffalo Valley, Putnam County. One night, an old railway employee, working under the bridge, slipped and fell, knocking himself out. Unfortunately his head was lying on the tracks when a train came along and decapitated the poor fellow. On a stormy and rainy night you just might see the headless man search for his head using a lantern. Is that why they call that bridge "Crazy George's Bridge"? If not, please let me know why it is called that.

ROBERTSON COUNTY

ADAMS

Adams is a small community in Robertson County and is home to the infamous Bell Witch. Much has been written about her but I will try to summarize it here for you.

John Bell was one of the first settlers in the area when, in 1817, a witch's activities were first noticed. Some thought it was a local eccentric named Kate Batts. There was dispute between John and Kate over the price of a slave that Bell sold the Batts woman. He was accused and tired for the offense and excommunicated from his church. Kate also claimed to have put a curse on John. Soon after, John saw a strange animal in his garden and took a shot at it. The creature disappeared. Then his children began to see bizarre things in the woods. His house began to shake and loud noises like that of windows rattling were heard there but nowhere else.

One year later, John Bell fell sick and told some friends about the troubles. His friends experienced the same phenomena when they stayed there. Word got around and many people came to investigate the situation. Then the unseen Witch began to talk and talk and talk! She harassed the John Bell and his family, except for his wife and John Jr., both of whom she seemed to like, making life miserable for the rest of the family.

Then John Bell drank a strange liquid, sicken and died. When some of that liquid was given to the family cat, it died immediately. The Witch, in a disembodied voice, bragged about what she did and said nasty things at his funeral.

In 1821, the Witch announced that she was going away for awhile but would return in seven years. And return she did but caused little commotion. Shortly there after, she said she was going away again and would return in one hundred and three years which would have been 1935. Came 1935 and no one noticed her if she did return. That is the basic story of the Bell Witch.

Ii is speculated that the long gone Bell Farm is still being haunted not only by the Bell Witch but also by John, Lucy, and Betsy Bell. The Bell Witch is even said to haunt a nearby cave, aptly named the Bell Witch Cave. What else?

In addition to the Bell Witch, mysterious lights have been seen on some railroad tracks and nearby woods in Adams. Some people feel they are related to the Bell Witch but others say a railway worker was decapitated on the tracks and now walks the tracks with a lantern looking for his long lost head. Other people believe that the lights have something to do with the Native American burial mounds common in the area.

RUTHERFORD COUNTY

Somewhere in Rutherford County there is a haunted Railroad Crossing. The Florence Road Railroad crossing, just off of Highway 70, has been the site of many tragic accidents and deaths. Some of the people killed at the crossing are said to be buried in a cemetery near that spot. The haunting is not apparently by any of those dead but supposedly by a man whose body was never found. In 1980, a young man was in love with a woman already engaged. When she would not break off her engagement to the other man, this young man vowed to throw himself in front of the next train to pass by on Halloween. A crowd gathered to watch him keep his threat but did not believe he would go through with it. A train did come by and he did jump. But, strangely, his body was never found and he was never seen again. Now, late at night every Halloween, the ghost of that scorned lover jumps to his supposed death.

BIG SPRINGS

Big Springs, a small community in Rutherford County, is just south of Murfreesboro. Strange things are said to have happened at the New Hope Baptist Church established in 1846. In the 1880s, the preacher in a revival held in the church summoned fire from Heaven. Guess what? Fires along with a giant barrel is said to have fallen from the sky terrifying everyone. Many felt that the Wrath of God had been brought down on the church, possibly because of a murder by a church member years before. He had killed a drifter and stole his money. Feeling guilty, he donated the "blood" money to help build the church building. Thus, in God's eyes, that was sin and now the church was cursed. Now mysterious lights are seen in the building late at night. Then one Wednesday night, lights fell from the sky just after a meeting. The disembodied crying of a baby can be heard. It is claimed that if you go into the graveyard and touch a tombstone, the baby will stop crying. There is even a headless ghost roaming around the property. In 1901, the old church was replaced with a new one and the strange happenings apparently ceased.

MURFREESBORO

The Stones River flows through Murfreesboro, a city in and the county seat of Rutherford County. Many bizarre events have occurred there since a Civil War battle was fought there in December, 1862. The Stones River Battlefield is a national park, and is haunted. At night, the ghosts of soldiers march and shoot at each other. You can hear the gun shots and the sound of marching feet. Sometimes the phantoms of long dead solders walk around the park.

Stop Number Two, aka the Slaughter Pen, is said to be the most haunted. Cold spots abound there and at the Wilder Watch Tower. Visitors to the Slaughter Pen have experiences feelings of paranoia and of being followed by unseen things or people.

ROCKVALE

Three women, accused of being witches in the 1800's, were executed and buried in the Dyer Cemetery at Rockvale in Rutherford County. Of course, the place is well and truly haunted. Beware of the cedar tree at the main gate. people have reported that they felt unseen hands like broom straw scratching their faces and arms. Balls of fire, the size of soft balls, are often seen in the center of the graveyard and going up the cedar trees where they then go out. Disembodied voices have been heard and full body apparitions have been spotted at the back of the cemetery. Usually, the ghosts are more active in the spring and fall.

SYMRNA

The Fate Sanders Recreation Area at near Symrna in Rutherford County is haunted by a little boy who steps out of the woods, laughs and ask for help in finding his father. I guess no one was able to help him.

SMITH COUNTY

BILLY HOLLOW ROAD

Many years ago, a small private plane crashed between Billy Hollow Road and Dean Hill

Road and all four passengers and the pilot were killed. Two of the dead were a mother and a baby. Now after dark the mother is often seen on road looking for her baby. Some people have also reported passing five strange looking people on either side of the road road but when they looked back for a further look, the people had disappeared as if into thin air. Disembodied screams have also been heard at night and mysterious lights spotted. A crying baby is also heard and even the frantic searching of the mother for the kid is said to also be heard.

LANCASTER

Lancaster is a small community in Smith County. A man once hung himself using a very long rope from a bluff approximately two miles from Center Hill Dam. His rescuers cut him down there at the bottom instead of climbing the steep bluff to the top and untie the rope. Local legend says that when there is no moon at night and you drive by that bluff, you will see the man hanging there. It is no use getting out of your car to get a better look as he will have disappeared by then.

STEWART COUNTY

DOVER

Dover is a city in Stewart County sixty-seven miles west-northwest of Nashville on the Cumberland River. The deserted run down mansion of Bellwood sits in the middle of a woods. It is supposed to harbor ghost, witches and other paranormal activity. I have however have not been able to find much else about it.

A Civil War Battle is apparently still being fought at the Fort Donnellson National Battlefield. Dead soldiers walk around the area at night and disembodied gun shots are heard in the darkness. The cemetery there is haunted by Civil War infantryman Reuben Hammond, who stands watch ensuring his dead comrades are not disturbed. He appears to be lonely as he follows visitors around and waves goodbye when they leave. The Crow Home in the middle of the city is rumored to be haunted by a man. Disembodied voices have been heard in the building and an occasional apparition puts in an appearance.

A Bed and Breakfast, once a hospital and sitting right next to the Fort Donnellson National Cemetery, has been the scene of paranormal activity. Doors open by themselves and soft crying can be heard throughout the building.

The Surrender House in Dover, part of Fort Donelson National Battlefield Park, is haunted the ghost of a Federal Officer.

There is a little traveled road near Dover where you have to pass through a nonexistent river! You can see and hear the flowing water but when you try to walk into it, you will not get wet.

SUMNER COUNTY

CASTALIANM SPRINGS

Cragfont Mansion is a historic building now housing a restaurant off Highway 25 in Castalian Springs in Sumner County. Cragfont, also known as the Winchester House, dates from 1798 and is thought to be haunted. At night, workers have have experienced the feeling of being followed by someone or something unseen, heard disembodied screaming and saw lit candles in the building when it was closed and empty. The ghost of James Winchester, the original owner, walks the house at night. It is also believed that his wife, Malvina, haunts the house. Both Union and Confederate soldiers, as well as slaves, also appear in the mansion. They may still give a Ghost Tour if you ask them.

GALLATIN

Gallatain is a city in and the county seat of Sumner County. Oliver's Restaurant was once upon a time the Sumner County Jail. There are reports of disembodied voices, footsteps and mysterious knocking on walls and slamming of doors in the upstairs area of the building late at night. Downstairs, the sound of toilets flushing and the water faucet being turned off and on can also be heard.

The mysterious disappearance of David Lang, a prominent owner of a horse breeding farm just outside of Gallatin, is still in contention today. Was he abducted by an invisible UFO as some claims or did he slip into another dimension or is the story just a story? On September 23, 1880, David Lang vanished into thin air, in the plain sight of his wife, children, brother-in-law, and a visitor named Judge Peck! Organized searches never found David or any evidence of what happened. There were no under ground caves or holes that he could have fallen into. He had vanished off the face of the Earth! Nine months later, when his children were at the spot where their father had disappeared, they found a circle of dead grass. One child walked into the circle and heard their father faintly calling for help. They rushed and told their mother who came out and heard her husband also. Sara, one of David's daughter, is said to have received a letter years later that read "help, help, help..." over and over in her father's handwriting. Supposedly David is still missing. What do you think happened to him if anything.

HENDERSONVILLE

Henderson is a city in Sumner County on the shores of Old Hickory Lake. Ellis Middle School, formerly Hendersonville High School, is haunted by a specter known as "The Colonel." Cleaning staff have heard footsteps in the upstairs hall at night when the place was supposed to be empty and a mysterious figure has been spotted in the second floor windows of the library. Many think the "Colonel" is Colonel Barry who used to own the property that the school sits on.

Mysterious sounds are often heard in Trinity Broadcasting Theatre at 44 Music Village Blvd in Hendersonville. People have said something about a man in black with long black hair was seen walking up to them but when they turned to look, he was not there. I am a little confused with this story. Why would they have to turn to see him when they reported that they saw him approaching them? Did someone else see him see him and tell the witness about him?

One Man's Treasure in Hendersonville was once an art business. A former owner/resident and her two children experienced a number of strange happening in the building. A door in an upstairs bedroom would open and close by itself even though the residents had to force it shut. Very loud knocking and scratching as well as a sound like the rustling of leaves could be heard in the wall of the middle room. Pictures were taken of woman's face and a large orb of bright light. Once a dozen pictures all fell off the walls downstairs at the same time. A roll of toilet paper unrolled itself in the restroom. It is said that pictures of the ghostly going-on's can be viewed at www.hauntedsouls. com. I will have to check that out.

SOUTH TUNNEL

South Tunnel is a small rural community near Gallatin. The train tracks that run nearby are not used as much any more. The community has a resident ghost known as the Lady in White of South Tunnel. She likes to roam around the nearby woods, the yard of residents and the train tracks. Pictures taken of her show a bright orb or glowing light. No one knows who she is and what she is doing there.

TROUSDALE COUNTY

I have not found any ghost stories for this county as yet. If you know any please email me at jamesfosterrobinson@live.com and I will include it in any future volume or revision. Type GHOST in the subject heading so I will not miss it.

VAN BUREN COUNTY

I have not found any ghost stories for this county as yet. If you know any please email me at jamesfosterrobinson@live.com and I will include it in any future volume or revision. Type GHOST in the subject heading so I will not miss it.

WARREN COUNTY

BLUE'S HILL

Devil's Cave can be found in Blue's Hill near McMinnville, the largest city in and the county seat of Warren County. It is not known how it got its name but a story told about it might give a clue. Two men were caving there some time again. One man let the other one down by rope. Then he heard a terrible scream coming from the cave and hauled the other man up. That man was shaking with fear, his hair had turned as white as snow and his skin was icy. He never did tell anyone what scared him. I guess that would be enough reason not to explore that cave.

WAYNE COUNTY

CLIFTON

The field behind the Public Library in Clifton, a city in Wayne County, may be haunted. A white figure of a man is often seen crossing the field between 8:00 PM and 5:00 AM. The ghost is thought to be that of one Rosco Young Blood looking for his money that he had buried in the field back in the 1950's.

COLLINWOOD

They tell about a possibly haunted tree in Collinwood, a small city in Wayne County, where slaves were hung during the days of slavery. On stormy nights, all of the trees except that particular tree sway to the winds blowing through their branche. It remains perfectly still.

WHITE COUNTY

I have not found any ghost stories for this county as yet. If you know any please email me at jamesfosterrobinson@live.com and I will include it in any future volume or revision. Type GHOST in the subject heading so I will not miss it.

WILLIAM SON COUNTY

FRANKLIN

The historical Carnton Mansion in Franklin, a city within and the county seat of Williamson County, was used as a Confederate hospital during the Civil War battle of Franklin. The battle seems to be still fought today with the disembodied sounds of rhythmic drum beats, running footsteps, gun shots and voices at night. Pictures of ghostly figures have been taken and recordings of the mysterious sounds have been made by local investigators.

Civil War soldiers are buried in the Carnton Plantation Cemetery. Twin brothers are buried in one row on the right. When people walk by that row of graves, it feels like someone is trying to tickle or grab their ankles. Many feel it it the ghost of one of the twin soldier brothers and not that of the little girl often seen in the graveyard.

The battle of Franklin took place around the Carter House. A number of ghosts haunt the house and grounds. Confederate soldiers can be heard marching down the hill to battle. The eldest son of Mr. Carter was injured in the battle and died on a bed in the house. He is seen there quite often. The ghosts of other wounded soldiers also appear in the building. The baby son of Mr. Carter who died when he fell down the staircase, likes to hang out in the Carter House.

The Confederate Cemetery next to Carton Mansion is haunted by a little girl who runs her hand along the fence as she runs up and down the fence row. Visitors have heard the eerie noise of her hand hitting the slats. A long dead soldier guards the graveyard, following visitors around until they depart the cemetery.

LEIPER'S FORK

Leiper's Fork, one of the oldest communities in Middle Tennessee, is near Franklin and the historic Natchez Trace Parkway. There are ghost lights in the area that bounce around near the historic district, through local fields and forests, and occasionally across the highway. Phantoms wearing nineteenth century style clothing have appeared on the side of the road usually after dark but occasionally during the day. Some locals feel that they are the spirits of early settlers but no one knows for sure.

WILSON COUNTY

LEBANON

Cumberland University is in Lebanon, a city in and the county seat of Wilson County. Mary White Dormitory is haunted by a girl who was killed by an escaped murderer. Because of the escape of the killer, residents were told to keep their doors locked. The murdered girl was supposed to give a secret knock when she returned from the common bathroom to the room she shared with a friend. The roommate did not unlock the door when she heard a knock as it was not the secret knock. Later she opened the door to see where her roommate was. The roommate was lying dead in the hall and blood was everywhere. Now that poor murdered girl haunts the hall and loves to play tricks. She turns TVs off and on. She trashes rooms, open and closes doors, pulls door knobs off as well as posters off walls. You get the picture.

Memorial Hall at Cumberland University has several resident ghosts. One is a boy who fell to his death while trying to sit in a third floor window. He now wanders the third floor having such ghostly fun as slamming doors in the hall. Some years ago, a teacher, who was leaving his classroom on the third floor one night, began to have chest pains. He died shortly thereafter at home. Visitors and students have remarked that when they were walking down from the third floor at night they felt like someone invisible was trying to push them. Maybe it is the ghost of that dead teacher trying to make them hurry.

Cedar Grove Cemetery in Lebanon has many well known Tennessee citizens buried there. Strange purple and white lights have been spied in the graveyard at night. No explanation has been advanced to explain the phenomena.

MOUNT JULIET

The city of Mount Juliet in western Wilson County is a suburb of Nashville about seventeen miles east of downtown Nashville. Where the Easter Seals Camp Lindahl is now located, an entire family perished in a house fire. The father, Mr. Cropper, now haunts the land apparently looking for those who set the fire. Interestingly enough, only the camp counselors see him.

WEST TENNESSEE

The boundaries of West Tennessee, one of the three Grand Divisions of the State of Tennessee, are the Mississippi River on the west and the Tennessee River on the east. All of Hardin County, bisected by the Tennessee River, has been included in West Tennessee.

COUNTIES

BENTON COUNTY

BIG SANDY

Big Sandy is a town in Benton County where a railroad conductor fell off his train and was beheaded near the Big Sandy Rail road Junction.

Now, on foggy nights and the anniversary of his decapitation, he searchs for his long lost head. If you are in that area at the right time, you will see a single light which will not move when you approach it. Apparently if you touch it, you will feel nothing.

CARROLL COUNTY

CLARKSBURG

Clarksburg's Palestine Church is abandoned and sits in the center of a graveyard. Some people have ventured into the church at night and have seen a person sitting at an old piano who would then start to play very low notes. The wood floor starts to creak as if someone unseen was walking on it. A figure wearing a black cloak covering their face also stands quietly in one corner. When they leave, they could hear something running through the woods. The church is supposedly unlocked and these mysterious folks could just be locals having a little fun. Maybe, but then maybe not!

HUNTINGTON

Huntington is a town in Carroll County and its county seat. There is a local legend that in the 1980's a woman working in the Huntington High School chopped off an woman's head and cooked it in the roast soup. The story further says that when ever the cafeteria staff makes roast soup, you can hear that poor woman crying out in pain. That would sure to be enough to turn you off roast soup.

McKENZIE

Chapel Hill Cemetery in McKenzie, a city at the tri-point of Carroll, Henry, and Weakley counties, is home to some strange lights that like to dance on top of the tombstones. Mysterious shadows of no known origin appear in a nearby church rebuilt on the site of an older one. Oh, yes! There is an old native American Mound nearby. Could it have something to do with the shadows? Only the "shadows" know! Sorry, I could not resist that.

CHESTER COUNTY

I have not found any ghost stories for this county as yet. If you know any please email me at jamesfosterrobinson@live.com and I will include it in any future volume or revision. Type GHOST in the subject heading so I will not miss it.

CROCKETT COUNTY

I have not found any ghost stories for this

county as yet. If you know any please email me at jamesfosterrobinson@live.com and I will include it in any future volume or revision. Type GHOST in the subject heading so I will not miss it.

DECATUR COUNTY

I have not found any ghost stories for this county as yet. If you know any please email me at jamesfosterrobinson@live.com and I will include it in any future volume or revision. Type GHOST in the subject heading so I will not miss it.

DYER COUNTY

DYERSBURG

Dyersburg Middle School in Dyersburg, the county seat of Dyer County, was the scene of a shooting in the gym of two teachers having an affair by the wife of one. in 1977. The wife died a few years after being sent to an insane asylum. The ghosts of those two ill starred lovers haunted that gym until it was torn down when a new school was built.

FAYETTE COUNTY

I have not found any ghost stories for this county as yet. If you know any please email me at jamesfosterrobinson@live.com and I will include it in any future volume or revision. Type GHOST in the subject heading so I will not miss it.

GIBSON COUNTY

MEDINA

There is, apparently, a lot of controversy about the Haunted Doll House in Hope Hill Cemetery in Medina, a city in Gibson County. A young girl died or was killed and her doll house was placed on her grave. The tale tells that if you see a light on in the doll house, the spirit of the little girl is playing in it. Of course, a number of people claimed to have seen the light and have looked into the windows and saw the little girl. The graveyard had no fence or gate and it became a favorite party spot. It has been said that the light was simply a bulb attached to a car battery that a former caretaker set up. Apparently, the vision of the light in the doll house caused all the partying to cease. Then a new caretaker built a house at the entrance to the cemetery and took out the light and the battery. Supposedly the light does not shine any longer in the haunted doll house. Do you know if it still does?

TRENTON

Sleepy Hollow, a small area of Trenton in Gibson County has a legend just like its big bother in New York State. Sleepy Hollow Lane is a rural road there and if you pull over to the side of the road, roll the window down and call out "Come to me!" three times, you just might be rewarded with the spectacle of many ghosts cavorting around the area and have your ears assailed by their ghostly moans. Don't be surprised if your car will not start until the sun comes up. You have been warned!

HARDEMAN COUNTY

BOLIVAR

Parren House can be found in the city and county seat of Bolivar in Hardeman County. The house had the name of "Wedding Cake House" and was owned by a man called Dave Parran, an undertaker. He liked to sit in a rocker on his porch and was loved and respect by everyone. When he died in 1936, his siting in his rocker on the porch was sorely missed by all. His rocker still sat there on that porch. Sometimes it would rock back and forth as if Dave was still in it. Then people began to see him in it and could hear him moving about his house. If Dave, the rocker and the house are still there, he is a a benevolent and well loved spirit.

HICKORY VALLEY

The Ames Plantation in the town of Hickory Valley in Hardeman County is haunted by the original owner's wife and daughter and others. Late in the evening, the disembodied sounds of slaves working and singing can be heard. The daughter and wife often appear dressed in old fashioned clothes.

HARDIN COUNTY

SHILOH

A great Civil War battle took place at Shiloh in Hardin County. In some respects, the battle is still be fought today by ghosts of long dead soldiers. "The Bloody Pond" is where injured and dying soldiers tried to slake their thirst. Their blood turned the water red. Those days, when the sun's ray hit the water of the pond just right, the water appears to be blood red. The phantom of a woman in a white dress often appears to female and children visitors who are sadden, frightened or lost in the park and tries to calm them down. She will readily disappear when someone else approached her and the person she it trying to help. She is thought to be the wife of one of the soldiers or officers that helped nurse the wounded at the pond.

Strange things like the opening and closing of doors and cabinets by unseen hands occurs in the old caretakers house at Shiloh National Military Park .

At Duncan Field, shadowy soldiers appear to be silently fighting the battle at night. They do not seem to notice the many witnesses who are watching their spectral battle.

HAYWOOD COUNTY

I have not found any ghost stories for this county as yet. If you know any please email me at jamesfosterrobinson@live.com and I will include it in any future volume or revision. Type GHOST in the subject heading so I will not miss it.

HENDERSON COUNTY

LEXINGTON

Lexington, a city in Henderson County, is midway between Memphis and Nashville, ten miles south of Interstate 40. Years ago a woman got hit by a car so bad that her head flew off. The car that hit her honked their horn three times just before they hit her. Then, apparently they stop, rolled down their window, got out and walked around their car five times wondering what to do, then got back in, rolled up their window and took off. Now, at midnight when there is a full moon, all you have to do to see her headless ghost, is just stop on the bridge, honk your horn three times, get out and walk around your car five times, roll your window up. Let me know if it works.

HENRY COUNTY

Hangings used to take place on, of course, Hanging Hill in Henry County. There is a branch that may or may not still stretch over the road by that hill. Local legend claims that if you park your car under the branch with the motor and lights off, you will see a light approach in the distance. It is supposedly the phantoms of people coming to watch the hangings.

PARIS

Dumpling Hill Cemetery, also known as Pleasant Grove Cemetery, is just outside of the community of Paris in rural Henry County. The place is haunted! A slave back in the early 1800's was convicted nad hung for some perceived crime and was buried in Dumpling Hill Cemetery. His ghost now roams the graveyard and some times chases any interlopers after dark.

There is a certain spot in a road in Paris that is apparently haunted. Stop your car there in the middle of the road and turn it off and a ghost will come out of nowhere and pound on your car. It is, they say, the spirit of a man whose car ran off the road and hit a tree and killed him. Now he wanders around searching for the things that he lost in the accident. Be carefull that you do not get hit by uncoming cars.

SPRINGVILLE

Springville is a small neighborhood town on a side road in Henry County. Years ago, a man was hung in the trees on a little dirt road off this side road. The Springville Ghost, as it is known today, appears as a swinging lantern coming towards those people who drove all the way down it to the dead end. The entrance is said to be chained to prevent entry and the property owner says he will not be responsible if anything happened to inquisitive thrill seekers. I suggest you talk to the owner first if you are serious about looking for this ghost light.

LAKE COUNTY

TIPTONVILLE

Margaret Newton Elementary School in Tiptonville, a town in and the county seat of Lake County, has a resident ghost. An unnamed female has been seen in the janitor's room and in the storage room. She is apparently not too fond of children as she has supposedly thrown chairs and brooms at the kids. It is not reported if anyone was injured by her antics.

LAUDERDALE COUNTY

I have not found any ghost stories for this county as yet. If you know any good stories please email me at jamesfosterrobinson@live.com and I will include it in any future volume or revision. Type GHOST in the subject heading so I will not miss it.

MADISON COUNTY

PINSON MOUNDS

The Pinson Mounds, a sacred place to Native Americans in Pinson Mounds State Archeological

Area in Madison County, is just south of Jackson. The spirits of long dead natives are said to haunt the place. Ghostly figures have been spotted and mysterious noises heard.

MCNAIRY COUNTY

PURDY

Purdy is a community three and one half miles northeast of Selmer in McNairy County. The Dodd House, down the road from the Purdy Cemetery, was the scene of a soldier's death in the Civil War. He was shot and died at the head of the stairs to the second floor. Now, on certain nights, his screams can be heard and blood reappears at the top of the stairs. Apparitions also put in an appearance and make a little ghostly noise at the Purdy Graveyard at night. Maybe they are having a party!

OBION COUNTY

I have not found any ghost stories for this county as yet. If you know any please email me at jamesfosterrobinson@live.com and I will include it in any future volume or revision. Type GHOST in the subject heading so I will not miss it.

SHELBY COUNTY

CORDOVA

Cordova is a community in Shelby County and lies on Memphis' northeast side, north of Germantown, and northwest of Collierville. The old Town Cemetery dates back to the early 1800's. Mysterious flashing lights of no known source are seen in the trees at night. The shadow of a face and orbs of light appear in photographs taken of a gravestone with the name "Susan" on it.

MEMPHIS

Memphis is a city in the southwestern corner of Tennessee and the county seat of Shelby County. A ghost known as the "Blue Lady" is said to rise up out of the water at Auburn Park and approach you when you park your car by the lake. An evil presence supposedly haunts the bottom floor of Memphis's Egypt Baptist Church. It is thought to be the reason that when someone approaches the church, there are lights reflecting on the windows from the light poles except for the four bottom ones which are completely black. Another church in Memphis is called the Fire Church. Day or night, nothing seems wrong with the building until you look at the back window. Many people have seen flames from a non-existing fire in that window. An army hospital used to be where the Metal Museum is now. Thousands died here from a yellow fever epidemic years ago. People have reported seeing things at night there and have experienced unspecified paranormal activity.

A room on the second floor of St. Jude Children's Research Hospital in Memphis is thought to be haunted by the friendly spirit of a seventeen year old girl who passed away there. The phantom of a lady in her thirties, wearing a long, light blue dress, often walks around the south side of the lake at Overton Park. If you approach her, she may stretch out her arm as if asking for help before she vanishes. She may be the ghost of a lady found murdered by the lake in the 1960's.

The ghost of a little girl, "Mary", haunts the Orpheum Theatre. She even has a favorite seat that she sits in whenever there is a performance put on. She sometimes appears by the organ and seems to like its music. It is widely believed that the ghost is that of a little girl who passed away in the fire that burnt down the original building.

Years ago, a young female student was said to have been raped and murdered in the old Blister Library tower at the University of Memphis. Over the years, custodians have seen a student in the building late at night only to see that student disappear into thin air. A disembodied scream of ""HELP ME!" was often heard by the campus police and others An unseen presence likes to ride the elevators in the UC Building. Set to automatically return to 2nd or 3rd floor if out of use for awhile, the elevator will open on the 1st or 4th floor instead. This ghost is thought to be the ghost of construction worker who fell from 3rd floor during the building of the student center and does not like that elevator to open on the 3rd floor. The building was demolished back around 2007.

The "Rose Room" in Memphis' Woodruff-Fontaine House at 680 Adams Avenue is haunted by Molly Woodruff. That room was once her bedroom. When not wandering about the house, she lays on the bed making a depression. Cold spots abound in the building. Back in the 1960's, when the house was opened as a museum, someone saw a woman in the Rose Room who told her that her bed does not go there. A strange odor like cigar smoke have been smelt on the third floor. I do not think that it is Molly smoking it. Must be a male ghost who is also hanging around the house.

The Brinkley Jar Mystery is one of the most well known ghost stories in Tennessee. For those of you who have never heard of it, I will summarize it here. Brinkley Female College, a prestigious women's school, is long gone today. Years ago, Clara Robertson, a thirteen year old student, experienced something very extraordinary and frightening on February 21, 1871. Looking up from her piano practice, she saw a girl with decaying fresh and wearing a moldy pink dress. Clara ran screaming from the room. No one believed her when she told them about it. As far as anyone knew there was only the ghost of the school's founder, Mr. Brinkley, haunting the place. The girl showed herself to Clara when she returned to the school a week later. This time the girl told her to dig under a certain stump outside the building and she would find a jar. Her father had some men dig there and , lo and behold, they found a jar. The little girl's ghost appeared once again to Clara and told her that since she herself did not find the jar, no one should open the jar until sixty day had passed. All involved agreed to it.

Local residents realized that Clara's description of the ghost fit that of Lizzie Davis who had died years before and had been buried in her pink dress when Clara had been three years old. How could Clara know that? This caused great interest and many people wanted to see the opening of the jar. Clara's father decided to do it in public and charge admission for people to attend the opening. But his plan was not to be. Her father was beaten one night and forced to reveal the jar's hiding place. The jar disappeared and was never seen again. Thought Clara never saw Lizzie again, she did talk to her during a seance years later.

Lizzie revealed that the famous Brinkley Jar contained a diamond necklace, some jewelry, $2,000 in gold coins and some "valuable papers."

Graceland, at 3734 Elvis Presley Boulevard in Memphis, is visited by millions of fans every year to see Elvis Presley's home. After Elvis died on August 16, 1977, people began to see him all over the world. Many felt that he was still alive while others were sure they saw his ghost. His ghost, of course, has been seen at Graceland. That is all I am going to say on the subject for now. I am a fan of Elvis but have not seen his ghost.

Libertyland Theme Park, at 940 Early Maxwell Blvd. in Memphis, is haunted by the kindly ghost of a carousel operator. Years ago, the kindly carousel operator went to recover a lost balloon for a child but forgot to turn off the machine. He was decapitated when it started up. Shortly there after, people started to see his spirit at the Theme Park. His ghost has been credited with turning off malfunctioning machine thus averting possible tragedies.

MILLINGTON

The school theater at Central High School in Millington, a city in Shelby County, is haunted by a ghost named "Herky". That was not the name of the woman when she was alive. If I was a ghost and given a name like that I would raise ghostly hell. I do not know if she did.

The Smoke Stacks in Millington used to be a gunpowder factory during both world wars. The building was mostly underground with a lot of tunnels. Local legend claims that an old insane, homeless man would kill and hide his victims there. The victims of the old man now haunt the surrounding woods while the old man himself hangs out in the tunnels.

A ghost known as the "Pigman" haunts Shelby Forest. His face looks just like a pig. When approached, he ups and disappears. They say there are others that haunt the woods but no one is saying who or what they are.

TIPTON COUNTY

ATOKA

The Bethel Assembly of God Church in Atoka, a town in Tipton County, has a large cemetery dating from the 1850's. A very unfriendly spirit with a lion sized body, dog like head and a coarse mane like hair, and deep red eyes haunts the graveyard. It does not like visitors after dark and will chase people out of the cemetery. If you can make it pass the fence, it will not chase you any further. Thank God for that!

MASON

Mason, a town in Tipton County is located along U.S. Route 70. A statue of the Virgin Mary behind the Old Trinity Church is said to bleed from the neck and eyes. It was the grave marker for a woman who passed away in 1912. The spirit of the person buried there supposedly bleeds or cries as some people believe because of the vandalism that has occurred in the cemetery over the years. Reports of unexplained lights and noises suggest that the place is also haunted. IT is strongly suggested that no one visit the place without permission.

WEAKLY COUNTY

I have not found any ghost stories for this county as yet. If you know any please email me at jamesfosterrobinson@live.com and I will include it in any future volume or revision. Type GHOST in the subject heading so I will not miss it.

REFERENCES

Internet
edu/~cadden/longautobio.html
http//en.wikipedia.
org/wiki/Grand_Divisions_of_Tennessee
http//en.wikipedia.org/wiki/West_Tennessee
http//en.wikipedia.org/wiki/East_Tennessee
http//ghoststoriesandhauntedplaces.blogspot.com/
http//www.hauntmastersclub.
com/places/greene_co_tn/tusculum/tusculum_colle
ge.html
http//markestglobal.com/
http//theshadowlands.net
http//utdailybeacon.com/
http//www.appalachianghostwalks.com/tennessee-
ghost-stories-haunted-places/harriman-ghosts.html
http//www.ghostsofamerica.com/states/tn.html
http//www.ghost-space.com/
http//www.ghosts.org
http//www.johnnorrisbrown.com/paranormal-
tn/index.htm
http//www.nashvilleghosttours.com/
http//www.people.fas.harvard

http//www.ryman.com/
http//www.suite101.com/content/haunted-places-in
-nashville-tennessee-
a285018#ixzz19YDB0FRmhttp//www.thehermitag
e.com
http//www.tnhistoryforkids.org/cities/nashville
http//www.uk-builder.com/blog/

Books, Etc
Austin, Joanne, Weird Hauntings/True Tales of
Ghostly Places, Sterling Publishing Co., Inc. 2006
Brown, Alan. /Haunted Tennessee Ghosts and
Strange Phenomena/
Southern Spirit Guide A Guide to the Ghosts and
Hauntings of the American   South Wednesday,
December 15, 2010 Southern Civil War Ghosts
        (Part III)
Price, Charles Edwin, Haunted Tennesee
Price, Charles Edwin, Mysterious Knoxville.
Daily Beacon Halloween Issue Fri Oct 29, 2010

SUGGESTED READING

Brown, Alan, Haunted Tennessee Ghosts and Strange Phenomena of the Volunteer State (Haunted Series) (Mar 30, 2009)

Coleman, Christopher K., Ghosts and Haunts of Tennessee (Feb 1, 2011)

Green, Thomas, Tennessee Ghost and Other Tall Tales, (Jul 15, 2013)

Haun, Charles, East Tennessee Ghost Stories, (Sep 5, 2012)

Kotarski, Georgiana C., Ghosts of the Southern Tennessee Valley (Jun 1, 2006)

Mott, A. S., Ghost Stories of Tennessee, (Sep 1, 2005)

O'Rear Jim and Brandon O'Rear, Tennessee Ghosts (Nov 1, 2008)

Price, Charles Edwin, Haints, Witches and Boogers

Russell, Randy and Janet Barnett, The Granny Curse and Other Ghosts and Legends from East Tennessee, (Oct 1999)

Thessin, Margie Gould, Ghosts Of Franklin Tennessee's Most Haunted Town (Apr 9, 2008)

ABOUT THE AUTHOR

James Foster Robinson was born in Ogdensburg, New York, USA but grew up in Prescott, Ontario, Canada. He has lived and worked in Ontario, Manitoba, Alberta and . In 2005, he moved to West Virginia and married his present wife, Betty. Jim has two books published by Mika Publishing, Belleville, Ontario Amazing Tales from Eastern Ontario, 1987; Strange But True Tales From Eastern Ontario, 1989. He has also published numerous articles in national magazines, daily and weekly newspapers. While living in Vancouver, BC, Jim was a Feature Writer on Suite101.com for topics - The Art of Storytelling, Storyteller's Korner, Sleep Disorders, Professional Security, and Liechtenstein. In addition, he was a Storyteller both in Kingston, Ontario and in Vancouver, BC,

Canada. James has also published "A Ghostly Guide to West Virginia", "West Virginia Weird and Wonderful", "An Encyclopedia of Lake and River Monsters", "Riotous Times, An Unauthorized History of Riots and Violent Protests in British Columbia, Canada", "A Ghostly Guide to Kentucky", "A Ghostly Guide to California", "The Wampus Cat, Myth or Reality", "Sleep Dancing With Death/Struggling with Sleep Apnea", "Storytelling for Fun", "Are They Ghosts?", "British Columbia Weird" and a children book "Tales To Tell My Children", a novel "Umpock - The Hole In The Ground", and his latest book "Ghost Lights, Spook Lights, Will o' Wisps and Friends" on Amazon.com. He is presently working on Ghostly Guides to the remaining 46 states and the 10 provinces of Canada.

www.ingramcontent.com/pod-product-compliance
Lightning Source LLC
Chambersburg PA
CBHW060518290526
45791CB00001B/434